Chile's Political
Culture
and Parties

RECENT TITLES FROM THE HELEN KELLOGG INSTITUTE
FOR INTERNATIONAL STUDIES

Scott Mainwaring, *general editor*

Roberto Bouzas and Jaime Ros, eds.
Economic Integration in the Western Hemisphere (1994)

Luca Meldolesi
Discovering the Possible: The Surprising World of Albert O. Hirschman (1995)

Mark P. Jones
Electoral Laws and the Survival of Presidential Democracies (1995)

Dimitri Sotiropolous
Populism and Bureaucracy: The Case of Greece under PASOK, 1981–1989 (1996)

Peter Lester Reich
Mexico's Hidden Revolution: The Catholic Church in Law and Politics since 1925 (1996)

Michael Fleet and Brian H. Smith, eds.
The Catholic Church and Democracy in Chile and Peru (1997)

Robert Pelton, C.S.C., ed.
Small Christian Communities: Imagining the Future Church (1997)

A. James McAdams, ed.
Transitional Justice and the Rule of Law in New Democracies (1997)

Carol Ann Drogus
Women, Religion, and Social Change in Brazil's Popular Church (1997)

Víctor E. Tokman and Guillermo O'Donnell, eds.
Poverty and Inequality in Latin America: Issues and New Challenges (1998)

Brian H. Smith
Religious Politics in Latin America, Pentecostal vs. Catholic (1998)

Tristan Anne Borer
Challenging the State: Churches as Political Actors in South Africa, 1980–1994 (1998)

Juan E. Méndez, Guillermo O'Donnell, and Paulo Sérgio Pinheiro, eds.
The (Un)Rule of Law and the Underprivileged in Latin America (1999)

Guillermo O'Donnell
Counterpoints: Selected Essays on Authoritarianism and Democratization (1999)

Howard Handelman and Mark Tessler, eds.
Democracy and Its Limits: Lessons from Asia, Latin America, and the Middle East (1999)

For a complete list of titles from the Kellogg Institute for International Studies, see http:www.undpress.nd.edu

Chile's Political Culture and Parties

An Anthropological Explanation

LARISSA ADLER LOMNITZ
and
ANA MELNICK

translated by Barbara Robledo

University of Notre Dame Press
Notre Dame, Indiana

Library of Congress Cataloging-in-Publication Data
Lomnitz, Larissa Adler de.
  [Cultura polâitica chilena y los partidos de centro. English]
  Chile's political culture and parties : an anthropological explanation
/ Larissa Adler Lomnitz, Ana Melnick.
    p. cm.
  "From the Helen Kellogg Institute for International Studies."
  Includes bibliographical references and index.
  ISBN 0-268-00840-x (cloth : alk. paper)—ISBN 0-268-02262-3 (pbk. :
alk. paper)
    1. Center parties—Chile.   2. Partido Radical (Chile)   3. Partido
Demâocrata-Cristiano (Chile)   I. Melnick, Ana.   II. Helen Kellogg
Institute for International Studies.   III. Title.
JL698.AI L6613   2000
306.2'6'0983—dc21

                                                  00-009919

This book is printed on acid-free paper

To my dear daughters-in-law:
Gale, Elena, and Norma
LARISSA

To my lovely family:
Husband, Children, and Grandchildren
ANA

Contents

Acknowledgments   ix

Introduction   *1*

1   Historical Background   *17*

2   Origins and Evolution of the Radical Party   *27*

3   Origins and Evolution of the Christian
Democrat Party   *47*

4   Party Subcultures   *81*

5   Conclusions   *141*

Bibliography   *149*

Index   *153*

Acknowledgments

The preparation of this modest book required several periods of reading and reflection, which led to the proposal of the general model and its application to Chile's history. One of the authors (LL) thanks to the Wilson Center (Washington, January–February, 1991) and to the WissenschaftsKolleg (Berlin, 1991–92) for their invitations, which provided access to specialized libraries and also the time and reflection necessary to elaborate the model, which in turn was the basis of the fieldwork in Chile. The Wenner-Gren Foundation provided both authors with the opportunity to do fieldwork and to process the information. We should also like to thank Nicolas and Ximena Weinstein, without whose affectionate hospitality and support it would have been impossible to complete the study. Finally, we should like to thank Mariana Aylwin and Sol Serrand for their ideas and enthusiastic support for this study.

Chile's Political Culture and Parties

Introduction

The aim of this study is to propose a model of political culture and to attempt to validate it by using Chile as a case study. This approach has the added benefit of offering a deeper understanding of the culture of political parties, a theme rarely considered in the literature on political parties.

THE MODEL

We understand culture to be a behavioral language composed of "grammar" (*la langue*) and "speech" (*la parole*). Grammar is the set of categories and rules representing continuity in culture, and speech is its linguistic behavior, which is, by its very nature, variable. The technological, economic, and political changes that occur in a society challenge the structure, and the result of this confrontation of conservative forces with those of change produce the society's history. The changes are interpreted and assimilated through the continuity of culture. Large and violent changes in cultural grammar occur during cataclysmic periods (conquest, wars, and revolutions). Otherwise, changes occur slowly; events gradually affect culture. People act, absorb, and assimilate change through a preexisting cultural grammar. That is what constitutes the dynamics of continuity and change.

Political culture is accordingly the grammar of relationships of domination/subordination/cooperation; that is, the grammar of social control and of power and how it is expressed.

We propose to define political culture on the basis of:

1. the structure of the social networks which are related to power and
2. that of the symbol system which legitimizes, nourishes, and supports that power.

1. The structure and function of social networks depend on the direction in which the exchanges take place—i.e., horizontal networks and vertical networks—on what is being exchanged, and on the articulation between networks. In every society there are symmetrical and asymmetrical exchanges, which produce horizontal and vertical networks. These networks interact among themselves to form the social fabric. The dominance of some over others and how they combine delineate the character of the political culture (e.g., authoritarian vs. egalitarian)

2. The symbol system, for its part, reinforces and legitimizes this structure of networks and includes such manifestations as discourse, political rituals, language, architecture, the myths of political cosmology, emblems, the use of time and space, and so forth, which are often integral to nationalistic ideology.

POLITICAL CULTURE

The concept of political culture is increasingly utilized in recent studies that attempt to understand and explain the nation-state, since traditional studies of political organization do not provide a complete vision of the system or of the bases of its identity. In other words, the cultural ingredient is increasingly being seen as a determining element.

The concept of political culture and interest in studying it arose out of the need to explain the dramatic sociological and political changes that occurred in Europe both during and after World War II. At first, elements of three intellectual perspectives (sociological, social-psychological and psycho-anthropological) helped take this theory in a qualitative direction. Later, the development of the quantitative methodologies of research through surveys helped make the study of political culture an independent subdiscipline within political science (see Almond and Verba, 1963).

This development led political culture theory to shift the emphasis from the subconscious elements—based on cultural aspects such as family structure, the relationships of parents and children and between sexes, primary and secondary socialization processes, attitudes toward authority, and so forth—to measuring the relationship between an individual's attitudes and expectations, toward the structure and the effectiveness of the political system (Almond, 1990: 138–54).

According to Almond, as he summarizes forty years in the subdiscipline of "political culture," the enormous number of studies would seem to have produced an "ambiguous" result: "on the one hand, political culture can change relatively rapidly; on the other, it would seem to be capable of resisting strong pressures without changing much" (149). "The data that we have on the stability and persistence of political culture suggests that political states of mind, such as confidence in the players and in the political institutions, appears to fluctuate, depending on the effective functioning of the leaders, and administrators and agencies. Basic political beliefs and values are more persistent, although they are also susceptible to change. Thus, for example, in the United States and Great Britain, in the '60s and '70s, although confidence in leaders and the political, economic, and social leaders dropped sharply, there was no evidence of a serious rejection of the basic legitimacy of American or British institutions, in spite of the poor economic and governmental display in both countries" (149–50).

The conclusion from this summary of the state of the question in political science is that political cultures are malleable and yet they persist over time. The authors recognize the problematic ambiguity here, namely a deficiency in theory growing out of what at the time was precisely its strength: the use of a sophisticated quantitative tools and the consequent neglect of an in-depth explanation.

Along these lines, Dittmer indicates that the dominant school of thought on this issue is that of psychological reductionism. Such reductionism facilitates the introduction of sophisticated sample survey techniques for measuring attitudes empirically. Recognizing the usefulness of these techniques for demonstrating that cultural patterns are not distributed uniformly throughout society and that not all members of society have an equal impact on determining dominant cultural patterns, Dittmer (1977: 555) emphasizes that "theoretical formulations should not be determined by methodological convenience alone)." He adds that methodological superiority vanishes when the social scientist researches cultures lacking in individualistic Western traditions (as for example, in the Third World) or where interviewing is not allowed (as in communist countries and a growing number of authoritarian systems): "if political culture can be reduced to the distribution of attitudes among a given population, what need is there for a conceptual framework and a distinctive line of research? Perhaps understanding a political culture is like learning a language: in order for the frequency distribution of vocabulary use to make sense, one has to have a basic understanding of the underlying grammatical structure" (Dittmer, 1977: 554–55). Pye agrees, using a different metaphor: "the situation is analogous to our capacity for saying *something* about the appearance of a building because we know what the elements are that are going to be used in its construction; however, to *represent* the building properly we have to also be aware of the plans and the overall design" (Pye in Dittmer, 555). Taking all this into account, we propose to use an anthropological approach that offers a different definition of political culture, and a methodology that allows us to study political culture in complex and modern societies.

SOCIAL AND EXCHANGE NETWORKS

Social networks are abstract constructions defined by re-searchers according to the criteria that interest them. That is, these relations are determined by some underlying criteria, making it possible to identify social structures that generally are not formally defined by society and that would not other-wise be identifiable. What is of interest to the social scientist is how the relationships are ordered, how the conduct of individu-als depends on their place in this order, and how the individuals themselves influence the ordering.

Thus a diagram can be drawn of the relationships where goods and services are exchanged, or of communication be-tween individuals, such as the exchange of administrative bu-reaucratic favors, of material loans or information. The ex-changes can be of three kinds: (a) reciprocal exchanges (between individuals with similar resources or lack thereof in a context of sociability or "trust"; (b) re-distributive (patron/client) ex-changes, that is, those between individuals of different status with unequal resources, typically power relationships set within personal relations where loyalty is exchanged for protection; and (c) market exchanges, where the circulation of goods and services is effected through the market and its laws (Polanyi, 1957: 234–69). Reciprocity and redistribution represent infor-mal forms of exchange, which are socially and culturally regu-lated, dating back to the origins of human society. These re-lations and the forms of exchange vary from culture to culture, both in the definition of the "partners" in the exchange as in what is susceptible to exchange and in the socially accepted ways of doing so. Hence, there is a social structure within which these exchanges take place (vertical and horizontal social net-works), the material and moral objects of exchange, and a sym-bol system that reinforces the structure of the network and of the society where this is occurring.

In complex societies an individual must deal with all three kinds of exchange (reciprocity, redistribution and market), and hence must participate simultaneously in three types of social relations, namely those of trust, hierarchy and class (see Lomnitz, 1975, 1987, 1988, and 1991). The economic, political, and socio-cultural domains become intertwined in the individual's life and their pattern shapes macro-social reality (Radcliffe-Brown, 1952; for the relationship between vertical networks and power, see Blau, 1964). Each form of exchange has rules that the individual learns to handle and—when they are contradictory—to reconcile with one another in each situation. Because this process is rich in symbolic language, the ability to handle symbols accordingly becomes a resource.

The resources exchanged determine and originate characteristic social structures. Mexico and Chile can serve as paradigmatic examples. In Mexico we observe vertically structured sectors crossed by horizontal networks. Capital and power are expressed through visible structures that have concentrated around them groups of individuals hierarchically ordered according to the level of resources to which they have access. Patterns of loyalty, life-styles, ideologies, and subcultures are formed through these hierarchies. Horizontal networks of reciprocal exchange are integrated into the vertical structures, thereby easing the pressure on hierarchical relationships and giving them flexibility. The structures or networks formed at personal levels ultimately tend to find expression in the national political system. Horizontal networks, if they are the dominant ones, crystallize in political parties of a horizontal variety with leaderships of a certain kind, while vertical networks in turn generate a different type of society. Mexico is a state with a corporate, vertical, authoritarian, and strong presidential system (a hierarchical society akin to a caste society, where the patriarchal, three-generation family exercises control over its members). Chile is a multiparty country, within which there are cohorts or horizontal groups of friends (who informally exercise a certain control over their members and create invisible boundaries setting them apart from others), in which leadership is under constraints; the result is both a strong presidential system based on an almost fanatic legitimacy, combined with factionalism and a strong parliamentary system. The entire system depends on ongoing horizontal negotiations. It is a society that is informally organized in horizontally structured social classes. In our opinion, the basic model for the make-up of each society is that given by the primary institutions that are the basis for sociability and social control. These are what give character to its political culture: in Mexico it is the authoritarian and vertical patriarchal family, whereas in Chile it is the group of friends. In the case of a nation-state, it would be the socially and culturally dominant group that puts its imprint on national institutions.

Our preliminary studies of the middle class (Lomnitz, 1971) suggest that, in Chilean political culture, horizontal relations prevail over vertical ones within the social classes and that this is reflected in its political organizations. That is, while there does indeed exist a widespread network of reciprocal exchange among members of the same class, narrower networks begin to concentrate until they formally produce political parties with internal exchanges of favors and communications, loyalties and resources, depending on the access that the party has to state power (Valenzuela, A., 1977). At the same time, within the parties, and linked to their growth, there arise cohorts or networks of friends from the same generation, the internal structure of these groups being egalitarian and highly emotional (such networks generally begin to appear among adolescents in the youth section of political parties). Within these friendship-based egalitarian networks—which by definition occur among equals—there come to the fore "natural" leaders, who are characterized in part by a permanent need and capacity for maintaining their legitimacy within the group. We could say that *if in Mexico the leader creates the group, in Chile the group selects and creates its leader.* Some of these leaders climb up through the primary network and reach higher ranks within the party, even reaching its highest leadership positions there, all the while having to prove themselves as leaders and being accepted by the grass roots. When this does not happen, splits take place within the party, factions are formed, and groups may separate to form new parties. The upshot is the *factional-ism* typical of Chilean political culture.

The well-known dominance of horizontal relationships based on trust would imply the possibility that access to power can be facilitated by structures more similar to horizontal net-works than to vertical hierarchies. Nevertheless, no complex social system can do away with the latter. Leaders are indispens-able, and this means that Chile faces a situation more difficult to resolve than that in Mexico, where the horizontal network is functional, and it complements and sustains the vertical hierar-chies. In Chile, however, hierarchy or leadership is something that runs counter to the ideal of horizontal network and the growth of parties. These contradictions are resolved—at the group level—by mechanisms inherent in Chilean political cul-ture: publicly making fun (*la talla*) of a leader who tries to in-flate his image or who shows little modesty, or directly putting him down (*el chaqueteo*), or removing him from his position by underhanded means ('cutting the floor out from under him') and so forth. At the same time, there is an emphasis on the need for leaders to be, and to seem to be, modest, austere, dedi-cated to the common good, legally correct, and above all, not to abuse their power. If a leader manages to consolidate his per-sonal power to the point of constructing his own vertical hier-archy, the system tends to erode this power, either by causing him to be defeated in the next elections, or through a split and the formation of dissident parties, leading to factionalism. When this has not worked, the system enters into a crisis, and sometimes the solutions that occur are authoritarian and un-avoidably based on physical coercion. The nature of Chilean political culture demands that both the horizontal and vertical dimensions be respected and accepted unanimously and legally. By contrast, in Mexico the predominance of the vertical aspect tends to concentrate power in the highest levels of society or directly in the president, and to consolidate all the political forces in one large party comprising very different sectors that negotiate among themselves within it. This authoritarianism is based on the country's political culture, and its structure of networks and the symbol system that sustains it and hence it can function without recourse to physical force. In Chile a monopoly of power in one party or individual would destroy the social peace that is based on a multiparty system of negotiations and alliances.

Thus, if in Mexico the horizontal style complements and sustains vertical hierarchies, in Chile, according to our hypothesis, hierarchy (or leadership) is antithetical to the growth of horizontal groups (parties), which would result in factionalism, a mechanism keeping hierarchic structures from taking hold and impeding the consolidation of a personal leadership, except for the legitimate leadership, subject to criticism, of the president of the republic. The resulting factions are generally composed of a small number of people representing a group of friends belonging to the ruling elite of the party (including young people, as this factionalism often expresses a generational conflict). Sometimes these factions grow and separate from the main body of the party to the point where they become significant parties with a large number of followers; this is the case with the Radical Party (which broke away from the Liberal Party) and the Christian Democrats (which came out of the Conservative trunk). In most cases, however, these factions end up joining other parties, or they survive for a while without having any significant effect. They might also disappear altogether (see for example Moulian and Torres, 1990; Edwards and Frei, 1949; Vial, 1981).

While factionalism is functional because it impedes leaders from accumulating too much power or hinders one party from achieving political hegemony that would allow it to govern without negotiation, an excess of factionalism leads to, or is an expression of, social and economic crisis. In some historical examples in Chile, authoritarianism has arisen in such situations (Presidents Ibañez and Pinochet). That is, the excess of factionalism pulverizes the system, the equilibrium of which depends on the existence of two or three basic parties, which encompass the main currents of thought into which in Chilean society is divided, and which are dependent on the class that they represent and/or their stance toward religion. It is these parties that, representing one or other of the main currents of thought, stand in continuity—under one name or another—and consequently in Chile there are parties that represent left, center, and right, and are both secular and Catholic (Valenzuela, Arturo, 1989; Valenzuela, Samuel, 1995; Scully, 1995: 136 and passim). How can we explain the continuity of this pattern over time?

We would say that, just as with ethnic groups or minorities belonging to the same nation, this continuity results from a combination of social networks comprising individuals occupying the same economic niche or sharing a common subculture. In the political system, the parties represent sets of social networks of individuals occupying specific economic and social niches that develop and consolidate common life-styles around a shared political ideology. Like the ethnic communities or minorities that make up a nation, political parties create symbolic boundaries that distinguish them from each other, and that make them feel different from the rest—what Fredrick Barth (1969: 14) defines as "we-ness"—and that are expressed not only in political ideologies but also in preferred lifestyles, forms of entertainment, the schools and universities to which they send their children, occupations, and so on. In other words, political parties represent characteristic subcultures which guarantee their continuity.

It should be pointed out that emphasizing the predominance in Chile of the horizontal over the vertical is not equivalent to claiming that society is not hierarchical, because political parties are generally organized on a class basis, and class differences are clearly established within the country's social fabric. What we are discussing is a model to be applied as an explanation and understanding of the political culture of a society, its origin and the continuity of its "grammar." In Mexico, the primary structure (the large patriarchal family) and the small vertical patron/client networks vertically articulated among themselves, issue in a corporative and presidential political system. In Chile, the political parties come together out of the horizontal networks of groups of friends, and this results in a society that is class-based and hierarchical, but not authoritarian. In Chile what we see at a macro level is a horizontally organized, although stratified, society (but one that is not impenetrable) deriving from the previously mentioned subcultures. In short, the basis of these subcultures is social class, but social class is defined by a mixture of variables including not only the individual's position in the economy but also the social networks within that class, the issue of religion, and ways of life. This is all quite obvious, for example, in the way people speak, and hence it is quite characteristic of Chilean society.

In such a system, characterized by its ability to contain strong political subcultures, it is very important to guarantee their coexistence, and that entails accepting a shared regulatory framework: the law. Such respect for the law, expressed in the constitution, is what *legitimizes* the system and presidential authority. This aspect of Chilean culture has been present from the beginning and is perhaps one of its best-known characteristics.

This finally is what we call a social grammar or culture: the social categories, the rules in effect, and each person's ability to function within them; grammar and speech, the primary structures resulting from them; and the political organizations into which they crystallize and through which access to power is obtained and exercised. These are what give national culture its character. Of course vertical and horizontal relations exist in all societies. What makes each society different is the mixture and combination of these ingredients and the relative importance of each kind of structure.

These ideas serve as the context for our study and analysis of the Radical Party and Christian Democrat Party in Chile, in which networks of friends, united by a horizontal type of ideological and social affinity, were quite obvious from the outset.

STUDIES OF POLITICAL PARTIES

Studies and analyses of political parties have had a long history. In his great work, *Partidos y Sistemas de Partidos*, Sartori surveys the literature on this theme from the eighteenth century onwards and proposes that a political party be defined as "any political group identified with an official label which presents itself for elections and can provide candidates for public office through elections (free or otherwise)" (Sartori, 1980: 91). From the perspective of the political system as a whole, the parties have an "expressive" function and a control function. The former is that of transmitting demands and pressuring that they be met. This implies the existence of a group of parties competing with one another in such a fashion that the citizens may turn to another party if the one they initally prefer does not satisfy their expectations. Sartori believes that where there is no party competition, or where there is only one party, one cannot speak of a party system, but only of a state-party system. On the other hand, competition between parties for the preference of citizens makes it possible for the party system to maintain control over the state (57–59, 82–83).

Sartori's most important contribution is the categorization of the party systems, which was to become the inevitable starting point for future research. The criteria that he invokes are as follows: (1) the number of "important" parties, resulting in one-, two-, or multi-party systems; (2) ideological distance, which accounts for the division of multi-party systems into polarized and moderate pluralism; (3) the existence of a party which outweighs the others, leading to predominant party or hegemonic party systems; and (4) the nature of the regime: one-party or hegemonic party systems are not competitive, while others are (Sartori, part 2).

Panebianco (1990) studies the internal power structure of the parties as organizations. "Power is a kind of asymmetric but reciprocal relationship which is manifested in an unequal exchange where one player gains more than another " (64). The tilt of negotiations between the actors depends on the level of control that they have over the areas of key uncertainty within the party.[1] Although leaders control the zones of crucial uncertainty, every party activist has control over some area of uncertainty, however small.

Panebianco distinguishes between "horizontal" power maneuvering (between leaders and followers) and "vertical" ones (among leaders within the same party). In the former there is an exchange of organizational incentives according to the specific kind of participation by party activists so as to allow as wide a mandate as possible. The greater the freedom of maneuver (power) obtained by the leader, the greater his ability to maintain the stability of an organizational order and resist the attacks of his adversaries in the minority elites. Negotiation in "vertical" power maneuvering depends therefore on the results of the negotiations in the horizontal power games (note the different use of the "horizontal" and "vertical" from the model previously presented).

Another important contribution by Panebianco is the model of the processes leading to the institutionalization of parties. He distinguishes four types of transformations: (1) From a system based on solidarity, guided by purposes shared by all members (cf. the first network in our model), to one based on interests and aimed at survival and mediation between objectives and heterogeneous demands; (2) from a manifest ideology to a latent one, where the incentives go from being predominantly ideological to predominantly material [again, see what has

---

1. Zones of uncertainty are those vital areas of the organization that, if not satisfied, would place it in a situation of uncertainty. The main zones of uncertainty are: (1) competition—the possession by one of the actors of a specialized knowledge which the rest see as being indispensable; (2) the relations with the environment, given the organization's limited control over it, and from which destructive challenges can arise; (3) communication—the ability to manipulate information; (4) formal rules—the ability (or inability) to establish, interpret, and force respect for the rules; (5) financing—contact with external sources of financing by particular actors; (6) recruitment—decision-making power over who may or may not belong to the organization and who, by fulfilling which requirements, will have a career in certain branches of it. (Panebianco, 1990: 83–88).

happened in Chile]; (3) from a strategy of control over the environment to a strategy of adaptation to it; (4) from a phase of maximum freedom of action on the part of the leaders to another where this is restricted as much as possible (309–10).

Applying these to Chile, we can conclude from the study to follow that political parties are indeed experiencing the four transformations mentioned by Panebianco. It is still not clear whether this process will inevitably lead to the institutionalization of the parties or to a crisis and possible decay, because change undermines the value-laden purposes that led to the establishment of the party, and ultimately, to the emergence of a contradiction between the party's distinctive we-ness and its "institutionalized" political actions.

For Latin America as a whole, Mainwaring and Scully (1995) have compiled a collection of articles on the institutionalization of the party system in various countries. In their introduction they emphasize the central importance of political parties in the political process and their function as the main means for attaining power. This importance is grounded in the parties' role as a symbolic point of reference used by citizens in getting their bearings in participation with minimal costs in terms of time and information and by party elites for attracting electorate.

The authors see institutionalization as the process by which a social practice or organization is established and recognized, even if not universally accepted. In institutionalized systems, social actors develop expectations, direction, and behavior based on the premise that this social practice or organization will prevail in the future. Citing Huntington (1968: 6), Mainwaring and Scully assert that institutionalization is the process by which organizations and procedures acquire value and stability (4).

A party system is institutionalized insofar as: (1) the rules and nature of the competition between parties are stable; (2) the most important parties have firm roots in society; (3) the principal actors offer legitimacy to the electoral process and to the parties, accepting that these determine access to power, and (4) the parties attain value in themselves and a status that is independent of, and autonomous from, the leaders and other organizations. By these criteria, Latin American countries are classified, according to the level of institutionalization of their party systems, in the following manner: institutionalized party systems (Chile for example); embryonic or weakly institutionalized party systems; and, as a residual category, hegemonic party systems in transition (as in Mexico).

In an institutionalized system, the parties participate in the structuring of the political process. Their actions are aimed at attaining power by peaceful and democratic means. When citizens have the information to evaluate candidates and their parties, those who govern can be held accountable to the governed, thereby legitimizing the system and facilitating governance through ways of handling conflicts that do not undermine authority (Mainwaring and Scully, 1995: 24–25).

Through these authors and the works of their followers we can appreciate that the key themes in the studies of party politics are the structure of the system and the internal organization of the parties. Recently, attention has been drawn to the importance of cultural aspects for better understanding the nature of parties and political systems in general. For example, the Mexican anthropologist Jorge Alonso (1996) defines political culture as "the sentiments, beliefs and values that provide significance to the political. In some fashion, it has to do with varying ethos surrounding power relations" (193). Parties, continues the author, do not include all that is political culture, "but mark its embodiment" (ibid.). With regard to the political culture of parties, Alonso notes the contradiction between the image presented by the political parties to the outside and that presented to the inside. This tension is expressed in discussions that are real as opposed to apparent, and in the difference between party programs and their pragmatic behavior. A party delimits its political culture and distinguishes it from others when it sets its objectives and defines and situates its adversaries. The ideological character of the party is defined by the interaction between theoretical considerations and actual practices. Its expressions in turn, arouse sentiments made up of both reason and passion (191–94). Likewise, parties contain transformative elements which are transmitted to society. "In inter-party and intra-party struggles, habits, life styles, and bureaucratic styles are developed, thereby establishing the relationship between governors and governed" (194).

As we delved deeper into the study of Chilean political culture through the model described at the beginning, the theme of political parties became more prominent. As Garretón says (1993: 224), political culture consists of the relationship existing between the state, the party political system, and society. He also states that the themes of meaning, language, forms of shared life, communication, and creativity (that is, culture) are indispensable for the understanding of political culture, including the political party system.

In conclusion, although the theme of the culture of political parties has begun to emerge during the past decade, there have been few (if indeed any) studies investigating the subject in depth through an ethnographic field study. This has been one of the aims of this book.

I

Historical Background

Before the appearance of the first political parties in Chile in the mid-nineteenth century civil political society was composed of an aristocracy united by family ties and friendship. According to Edwards, it was this aristocratic fronde [*fronde aristocrática*], which in fact decided who would be president, was the direct predecessor of these first parties (Edwards, 1928; 1982 edition: 34, 80). This fronde, as Edwards describes it, coincides with what we call a horizontal network, consisting of friends from the same families and linked by bonds of family relationship and friendship. The origin of this fronde goes back to colonial times, when there already existed an homogeneous native-born aristocracy almost entirely concentrated in Santiago that unquestioningly accepted Spain's tutelage. When Bonaparte usurped the throne, they and the Spaniards decided to oppose this usurpation which threatened the whole principle of legitimacy. Nevertheless, the Spaniards saw it as a transitory event, while the native elites, refusing to accept a situation they considered illegitimate, began to think of permanent independence. Hostilities arose between the two groups, which already differed culturally and in their ways of life. The aristocrats had a low opinion of the new arrivals from overseas, who, from the mere fact of having been born in Spain, enjoyed many privileges, while the Creoles were landowners and had both education and rank. They were the "aristocratic fronde" (ibid.: 47–50). When they heard that the

Regency had chosen a Spaniard as the new president of Chile, there was a strong political reaction rejecting this President on the grounds of his lack of legitimacy. This led to war, and the fronde had to resort to military forces concentrated in Concepcion. Military strongmen came to the fore, and General Bernardo O'Higgins, leader of the struggle for independence, took command of the nation. Says Edwards: "O'Higgins attempted to organize the country under a Caesarist [absolutist] regime, but in spite of his strength and prestige, he was unable to establish stability. The Santiago *fronde* soon brought him down" (53). O'Higgins was unable to get along with the ruling class, who did not want another monarchy (least of all one lacking social legitimacy) or Caesarism, and hence he was isolated and forced into retirement. There followed years of intermittent, unstable and anarchic Caesarism (until the 1829 Revolution, the age of the *"pipiolos"* (members of the Chilean Liberal Party). But "the arrogant Chilean masters wanted to be taken into account and to have control, or at least an organized regime with influence shared among the prominent members of the social family to which they all belonged. They were in continual confrontation with the power and ambitions of the military commanders" (59). Edwards believes that this aristocratic fronde was what kept Chile from undergoing long periods of military rule and chaos. They wanted peace, a legitimate republican government with a president selected from their midst, and protection of their interests. However, they were not willing to accept a leader who was military or personalistic, or from another social class.

At the beginning of the struggle for independence, the kingdom of Chile was Spain's most compact colony, with a homogeneous aristocracy, and only one important social center—Santiago—where wealth was concentrated and where the upper classes, the magistrates, and the higher ranking civil servants lived. In Concepcion there was also an aristocratic group, one that was poorer. Concepcion was the military center since it was close to the border with the kingdom of Araucania, while social influence, cultural traditions, and administrative expertise were all concentrated in Santiago. We could say that Chile's national identity was consolidated before independence, with no need for a conscious nationalist movement, such as those in Europe in the eighteenth century or in Mexico in the early twentieth century after the revolutionary period. That is why Chilean nationalist discourse is a considerably less explicit manifestation of Chilean identity.

Various historians (Edwards, 1982; Góngora, 1981; Vial, 1981) agree that the creator of the Chilean nation-state was Portales, who invoked the legal principles of earlier times. According to Edwards, Portales' primary accomplishment was to restore the feeling of what had served as a basis for public order for three centuries of colonial rule: the existence of a strong and enduring power, superior to the prestige of a military strongman or the force of a particular group: "the sentiment and the habit of obeying legitimately established governments" (Edwards, 1982: 66). Góngora likewise says that the state at that time was expressed in Enlightenment terms: its aim was "the common good" and "good government." After a brief period of chaos (1823–30), the national state remained consolidated for a long time (Góngora, 1981: 12). It was shaped by the thinking of Diego Portales, which consisted of restoring the idea of unconditional obedience (previously to the king) to whoever exercised legitimate authority, because such was the law (13).

The horizontal networks that later were to find expression in the "aristocratic fronde" were established early in colonial Chile. They were aided by the history of the conquest, the characteristics of the conquerors and the indigenous groups, the small size of the colonized territory, as well as the scarcity of mineral resources (silver and gold), which made Spain little interested in imposing a firmly authoritarian system on this very distant territory. What Portales did was to restore the principle of "authority." According to Edwards, "by 1830 there was already a strong and solid power, without the name of a caudillo, and with the features in both substance and style that could win the sympathies of the powerful: legal regularity, decorum and circumspection, silent and quiet strength, respect for tradition and interests, the assurance of order and good government. For many years the two specters of O'Higgins' Caesarism and anarchic chaos kept society tranquil around an impersonal government, political tradition, and legal order" (Edwards, 1982: 75).

Nevertheless, Góngora states that Portales' regime was neither impersonal nor abstract, but rather that the government needed the support of the landowning aristocracy, which in turn had to subject itself obediently to government for the sake of its own interest in public order. It was a polarity accepted by both sides: (1) an authoritarian government that intervenes openly in elections, sending provincial governors the lists from which the members of parliament could be elected, and (2) a landowning aristocracy opening up to civil servants and military men coming from the middle ranks. The Portales regime assumed that the aristocracy identified its social rank with the moral quality of preferring public order to chaos. "This is the mainspring of the Portales machine" (Góngora, 1981: 114–16). According to this author, what emerged in 1830 was a strong government quite different from the militarism and strongman rule of the Independence period, which in the 1833 Constitution declared Chile to be a representative democratic republic supporting the legitimacy of anyone elected through legal procedures and "governing the country according to these legal norms" (13).

This so-called *"pelucona"* (wigged, i.e., Conservative) Constitution established a system of presidential government with a two-chamber legislature, where the president of the republic and the senators were elected, and the members of the lower house were appointed by the executive. These elections, however, only involved single men of 25 years or older and married men of 21 and older who were literate and property owners or who had a certain amount of capital (Valenzuela, 1985: 7; R. Donoso, 1952; Scully, 1992: 43–44).

During the period from 1830 to 1850, "governments, although strong, were wise enough not to fight blindly against the powerful aristocracy, that had brought down the monarchy and Caesarism. The relations between presidential absolutism, tempered more or less by oligarchic 'opinion,' and the independent tendencies of the aristocracy, kept things in balance . . . until that balance began to be lost because the aristocracy—once the danger of anarchy was gone—was unwilling to grant unconditional support to the absolute power that had been rebuilt by one man (Portales), and the 'fronde' reemerged" (Edwards, 1982: 80).

EMERGENCE OF POLITICAL PARTIES

In Karen Remmer's opinion, the first political parties began to appear in the 1820s, although they were not exactly political parties but rather groups of friends or relatives united by common interests. "Rather than organized political structures, the political currents of thought that emerged as a consequence of the disintegration of the Spanish colonial authority were fluid coalitions between rival leaders, kinship networks, and local cliques" (Remmer, 1984: 10). These groups or "proto-parties " still required more than half a century to become consolidated as political parties: "none of the political groups competing for power in the 1870–1891 period formally existed outside of the legislature" (17). They were groups with some cohesion and durability that functioned on the basis of loyalty and solidarity, and whose members shared certain political ideals. None of them had the support of the masses or of any wide sector of society. Remmer states that by this time group factionalism, another feature of Chilean political culture, had appeared, and it did so as much within the Conservative aristocracy—the dominant political group until 1879—as among the Liberals, who were constantly afflicted by a chronic factionalism (ibid.: 14–15).

The first parliamentary fronde arose when the minister Camilo Vial filled the list of candidates for the new congress with members of his family, his dependents, and his proteges, ignoring the renowned figures of the time (ibid., 16). Such were the origins of the first Chilean political party, the Conservative Party. Factions then began to form, giving origin to a new stage in Chilean political life: horizontal social networks formally became political parties. As Edwards says, the liberal fronde emerged in parliament, but it was "events, and connections of family and friends, not principles, that shaped these men into a group. Simply erasing the Vials, the Errazurizs and close relatives of these Santiago tribes would have reduced them to nothing" (Edwards, 1982: 87). Góngora also notes that, at the same time, the aristocracy expanded with new groups: copper and silver miners, coal miners, "modern" farmers from the Aconcagua Valley, and foreign exporters (Englishmen and Irishmen with a speculative and financial spirit). The aristocratic family was no longer homogeneous, and along with this change came an anticlerical spirit (e.g., the miners from the north, such as Gallo and Matta). Part of the aristocratic fronde became ideological in the French manner and advocated a relaxation of the church-state relations, the restriction of presidential power, and universal suffrage for literate men of twenty-one and older (Edwards, 1982: 84–86; Góngora, 1981: 16–18). Thus arose the Liberal Party, in opposition to the Conservative Party, which continued to maintain an extremely Catholic ideology and a belief that church and state should be closely connected.

It should be mentioned that the Conservatives' permanent control over the government notwithstanding, economic and social conditions in Chilean society produced a number of major changes which exploded in the 1870s and had important consequences in the political terrain. Between 1871 and 1886 cemeteries, which until this time had been controlled exclusively by the Catholic Church, were secularized. By law special sections were now opened for the burial of non-Catholics (Vial, 1981, vol. 1: 93). Civil marriage was also established, and the church was deprived of the exclusive right to register births, marriages, and deaths (Remmer, 1984: 15). In addition, a massive plan for basic education was launched under President Montt, in keeping with the principles of secular positivism, thus supplanting the church as the only educational force in the country (Vial, 1981, vol. 2: 689; also Serrano, 1994). These changes came about not because the Conservatives gave in or the Liberals grew stronger, but primarily because other social forces resulting from a series of major economic developments began to make themselves felt.

The so-called "War of the Pacific," a watershed in Chilean history, broke out in 1879. As winner of the conflict, Chile took over the nitrate lands wrested from Peru and Bolivia, and with what it earned from them, Chile in ten years attained the highest per capita income in all of Latin America. This nitrate boom contributed to the appearance of new social classes in Chile. On the one hand, the new nitrate industry needed labor; on the other, it strengthened the new mining bourgeoisie in the North of the country—very different from the landowning bourgeoisie in the center of Chile. Most of all, it created a group of mid-level employees in the service sector who handled the administration and commercialization of nitrate. On top of this, there were new opportunities for work around the nitrate colonies for the so-called liberal professions: doctors, lawyers, engineers, and schoolteachers. Mixed into this new middle class were young aristocrats who, under the ideal of Comtian positivism, gave up their privileged position in order to dedicate themselves to a liberal profession, and small farmers who migrated to the urban centers to work in trade, transport, skilled trades, or mining (Remmer, 1984: 35–40). Another early component of the Chilean middle class was the foreign element—mainly English, German and French—who began to arrive in Chile in the mid-nineteenth century, bringing with them the ideals of secular and positivist education (Vial, 1981, vol. 1: 47).

In 1883 the military campaign against the Araucanian Indians ended successfully, thus giving rise to a new landowning bourgeoisie in the south of the country, who were to take over a large quantity of prime quality agricultural lands. The Pacific War, the nitrate boom, and agricultural expansion in the south all produced nationalist feelings which found expression in public education, where the ideal was the formation of the "national soul," in which the educated middle classes mediate between rich and poor. Religious educators began to be replaced by lay educators and a whole national secular teaching body was created and came to be called the "teaching state" (Vial, 1981, vol. 1: 121).

According to Vial, the national unity prevailing until 1870 was made possible by an agreement on the conception of life and accepted values to be taught, namely, Catholicism in its Spanish form. It was under these shared values that the aristocracy governed. Then, from 1860 on, the agnostic and irreligious generation born in 1825 came to the fore, and their lack of religious fervor became militant anti-Catholic sectarianism. For them the supreme virtue was freedom. These men included outstanding figures in education, science, literature, and politics, many of them educated in Europe. The fissure became a chasm that brought an end to national unity. The different bands were unable to destroy one another (in the War of 1871) but neither did they unite, and instead, they unleashed a great deal of personal violence. Sectarianism took shape in political parties, which came to be called Conservatives and Liberals (ibid.: 38–66; Góngora, 1982: 16–18).

In this instance we see how a horizontal group only accepts leadership in a conditioned form (while the leader maintains his legitimacy); how informal networks become political parties (the basis of the present Chilean political system); and how factionalism arises. Finally, this episode illustrates the appearance of the divisive currents of thought that still exist within the political parties. Here the issue is that of religion, which is emblematic of the two political parties that concern us: the Radical Party, which split away from the Liberal Party, and the Christian Democrats, which split from the Conservative Party.

As a direct precedent for this situation described by Vial, it is worth mentioning Cristián Gazmuri's observation in *El "48" Chileno* that the generation that went through the Chilean '48 and created the Society of Equality, also left an ideological legacy. "Liberalism that had been enriched in ideas was radicalized and constituted the ideology of the oligarchy's younger generation, which was to govern Chile starting in 1870, and would impose a liberal institutional framework; in short, what Alberto Edwards calls the 'liberal religion'" (Gazmuri, 1991: 113). He goes on to say that "The Society of Equality could consider itself, at least in its first period, as the first modern party to exist in Chile, and this represented a change in Chilean social patterns. As we shall see, this party was to take shape first as the Radical Party, then as the Reform Club, and finally, to a greater or lesser degree, in all of Chile's political organizations in the late nineteenth century (84). The "Chilean '48," says Gazmuri, marked a new type of "political sociability," which was to be expressed later in the organizational pattern of the Radical Party, and to a greater or lesser extent in all the political parties up to 1920. But the new form of group activity was not limited to the political sphere. "It appeared in organizations based on ideas and philanthropy: the Freemasons, the fire fighters, also copied from previous European and American patterns" (115). That is, a widening and diversification of the existing social networks eventually produced the new political party (or parties). As Gazmuri also points out, in stating the purpose of his study, it was a public elite formed during the period he studied, and it was the young oligarchs of the revolutionary movements of 1850–51 who projected their ideas until they became embodied in the institutions of Chile. Gazmuri adds, "It is possible that, were we to make a study of property based on individual persons, widening our area of study (family relationships, contexts, realities and patrimonial continuity) our conclusions would be much richer" (118).

In the process leading up to the formalization of a political party we can observe the expansion and settlement of the informal networks, uniting in a relatively homogenous fabric those bound by family or friendship ties. The qualitative change that Gazmuri calls the "shift of Chilean political sociability" marks the moment when an informal network or networks adopted a formal structure or organization.[1]

During the second half of the nineteenth century, splits from the Liberal and Conservative Parties led to the formation of the National and the Radical parties.

1. Gazmuri specifies that the newspaper, *The Tribune*, financed by Montt and Varas, uses the concept of "sociability" as "level of social development" and not as it is understood in modern historiography.

2

Origins and Evolution of the Radical Party

Edwards describes the group in opposition to President Perez that appeared around 1863 as "the Radicals, as this circle of intellectual combatants were beginning to be called, whose well-defined ideas were aimed at embodying the program of 'spiritual' Liberalism" (1982: 140). According to him, the Radicals were not yet a middle class party: "their leaders came from the social 'lions' of that time, more romantic than carefree, Victor-Hugo-style poets, happy destroyers of all the conventions, democrats, free thinkers, according to the latest model of the bourgeois moral revolution, many of them burning with progressive faith, the rest intellectually empty-headed" (ibid.: 152). It was an extreme version of Liberalism and is a direct predecessor of the Radical Party (PR).

There are three important historical moments in the formation and establishment of the Chilean Radical Party. First comes the appearance of Radical thought, as a sub-product of the enlightened Liberalism which influenced a group of young Chileans at the beginning of the nineteenth century. Then there was the establishment of a network of bourgeois friends, acquaintances and families, within a political group, with common interests, that took for their banner a not yet sharply defined Radicalism and that caused schisms several times even before the political party was established. Finally, there was the moment when the Radical Party began to act as a genuine political party in the early twentieth century, when its influence and its programs of action became more than the simple networks of friends, acquaintances, and family and began to receive support from a heterogeneous group of individuals, whose interests would be represented on the party's political platform.

What was called the "Radical" political tendency had its roots in France in the early nineteenth century, where there was in fact a Radical Party. Briefly the 'Radical doctrine' represented, in its time, vanguard thought of enlightened Liberalism, a product of the ideals of the French Revolution, seeking to establish a republic to replace the monarchy through universal suffrage for all (male) "citizens" in the country. Although some of the Liberals were Catholics and not openly opposed to the participation of the church in state affairs, most Radicals were anti-clerical and wanted a clear-cut separation of the church from the state and the establishment of a civil and lay state.

Radical ideas arrived in Chile by two routes; one was the immigration of Europeans who arrived in Chile during the nineteenth century, and the other was the young aristocratic Chileans who had studied in Europe and returned to Chile imbued with the ideals of enlightened Liberalism (Vial, 1981, vol. 1: 45). Also worth mention is the so-called "generation of 1825" composed of young men from well-off Catholic families who returned from France and Germany mainly as agnostics or atheists, with their Liberal university degrees and whose education embraced the ideals of the Enlightenment, Spencerian scientism, and Comtian positivism (ibid.: 102). Timothy Scully points out that the first Radicals were a group of Liberals who, indignant at the 1850 alliance of the Liberal Party with the Conservatives, decided to form their own group (Scully, 1992: 67). When President Manuel Montt became too involved in activities against the Catholic church (the beginning of secularism), he kindled discontent among the clergy and the Conservatives. Those Liberals who were opposed to the President took advantage of the opportunity and allied with the Conservatives against Montt. Liberals who were opposed to the idea of making decisions on personal grounds and considered the Conservatives as political enemies separated from the "unionist" Liberals and formed an independent political group with a "Radical" tendency.

In 1857, six years before the first Radical assembly in Copiapó, an armed conflict broke out that for some marked the beginning of Chilean Radicalism: the so-called revolution of the Gallos, in which an armed group commanded by Pedro Leon and Angel Custodio Gallo, who sympathized with "Radical" Liberalism, rose up against the Conservative government and its policies of extreme centralism and the excessive executive power (one more example of what is described as the horizontal characteristics of Chilean political culture). The rebellion, extended over several northern cities, was finally repressed everywhere but Copiapó (Sepulveda, 1994: 237). This armed conflict marked an important point in the history of Radicalism because it was the expression of a social sector, the mining bourgeoisie in the northern Chile, which was seeking representation in a government which had been until then exclusively for the landowning bourgeoisie. By the 1871 election, when Federico Zañartu was elected president, the Radicals appeared as a political group separate from the unionist Liberals, from the Nationalists, and of course from the Conservatives (Remmer, 1984: 14). According to Gazmuri, the beginning of the Radical Party marks the appearance of a new political form of sociability in Chile, promoting the dissemination and institutionalization of the French 1848 culture. In 1857 this group published the daily *La Asamblea Constituyente* and while still within the Liberal Party they became organized in opposition to the "Liberal-Conservative Fusion" which followed the crisis of the more old-fashioned Conservatism. As already mentioned, the opportunistic support by Liberals for the Conservative Party against President Montt proved to be unacceptable to those who saw the state's independence from the church as essential.

Gazmuri emphasizes that the Radical Party historians agree that this group of anti-clerical Liberals, later to be the nucleus of the new party, "not only had belonged to, but were the direct descendents, of the 'Liberal youth of the Bulnes period'. They were the descendents of our 48ers (Quarante-Huitards)," revolutionaries and francophiles. On the other hand the Liberals who were willing to merge with the clerical Conservatives, now distanced from the government, came primarily from the pro-Vial branch splintered from the *pelucones* in 1849 (Gazmuri, 1991: 130). As intransigent lay Liberals Gazmuri mentions Angel Custodio Gallo, Francisco Marin, Justo Arteaga, Luis Rodriguez Velasco, Santiago Cobo Alemparte, and Guillermo and Manuel Antonio Matta, the group's leader. The most salient features of Radical thought were a rational secularism and militant anticlericalism and a strong opposition to central control, all of which are expressed in the definition made by Manuel Antonio Matta in 1862 of the principles that inspired Radicalism in its early stages:

1. The Constitution should be reformed to remove excessive powers from the all-powerful executive, the source of immeasurable abuse.
2. Electoral freedom should produce "power" through universal suffrage which would block the demands of a privileged caste whose rights are derived "from the amount of their wealth."
3. Education must be secular, independent of any confessional control; this is not intended as an attack on religion, but on religious intransigence.
4. Pressure should not be put on conscience to gain members.
5. Local government law should place barriers to the centralized authoritarianism coming from the presidential palace ("La Moneda") (Gazmuri, ibid.: 132).

The exact date of the creation of the Chilean Radical Party lies somewhere in history and party mythology. Timothy Scully maintains that the first Radicals were organized about the 1850s (Scully, 1992: 64) and another author suggests the creation of the daily *El Constituyente* in 1862 as the starting point of Radicalism (Sepulveda, 1994: 237).

Gonzalo Vial (1981, vol. 1: 365) is of the opinion that 1863 can be taken as the year that the PR was founded, because the first Radical Assembly took place that year in the northern mining city of Copiapó. Karen Remmer, however, insists that the first Radical Convention which took place in 1888 in Santiago may be the real beginning of the Radical Party because that was when the first national convention took place, and it was there that an attempt was first made to define the party's political platform, its national structure, a work plan with concrete actions and the rules for election of Radical leaders in the entire country. (Remmer, 1984: 63–64)

As just mentioned, the first Radical Assembly occurred in Copiapó, despite the Santiago origins of the founding group. Their leader, Manuel Antonio Matta, came from this mining city, where he had wealth, relatives, and friends. When Matta returned from his exile in England, he and some others organized a group for political analysis and disseminating ideas in Copiapó. In 1862, this group created the so-called "Atacama Fraternity," which was intended to unite members of an informal liberal reformist party, the radical wing of the Atacama Liberal Party. In late 1863, this group became a center for political activism, and with eyes on the 1864 parliamentary elections, created an "electoral assembly." This was to be in fact the first "Radical assembly" in Chile (Gazmuri, 1991: 132) and the invitation was issued through an announcement in the newspaper *La Voz de Chile*. According to Gazmuri, this invitation marked the foundation of the Radical Party "with relation to the form of sociability which characterizes it par excellence—the 'assembly'"—a social form typical of the "societal" spirit and what Manuel Antonio Matta had already announced the previous year as the central element of the doctrine which had stimulated them, clearly separating himself in this aspect from theoretical Liberalism. In defense of the "societal" idea, Matta wrote: "Barbarism means isolation, the individualism of a person, a family, or a tribe, whose entire sphere of action reaches only as far as their arms or their weapons; hence it declines to the extent that such isolation wanes, withdraws, and gives way to its opposite—association. . . . The surprising effects of association accepted by all those called together, whether white or red, socialists or not, are the natural fruit, the essential consequence of this very social life." An attempt to put this idea into practice would be assemblies of urban clubs" (ibid.: 137). This was while the group still remained part of the Liberal Party. In 1863 there were already five Liberal-Radical parliamentary representatives. The most active and outstanding personalities involved in this "dissident" form of Liberalism were "provincial oligarchs, some of them very wealthy, Santiago oligarchs, as well as yet simple middle-class men with outstanding talents who had been acquiring political weight in Chile since the government of Jose Joaquin Perez (ibid.: 134).[1]

These rebellious forces represented a new cultural vision of the world, distant from the traditionalism and hierarchic social values recommended by Catholic conservatism. Thus, the explanation involves not only the emergence of a new entrepreneurial class, but also of the cultural element just described. The presence of these new entrepreneurs likewise played an important role in the birth of the new forms of sociability, whether political or not. Hence, the most important element of the 1851 movement and even more so of the 1859 one is that, despite their military failure, they consolidated the lay, anti-centralist, anti-authoritarian, anti-conservative tendency among these bourgeois who were to be Radicals—firemen, Masons or members of the Reform Club—and who from these positions were influential in promoting some of the structural changes that they desired, not in the sense of a "bourgeois revolution but rather of an evolution." In contrast to the Society of

1. In his stimulating study of the Chilean '48, Cristián Gazmuri probes the causes of the 1851 and 1859 revolutions, usually attributed to the rise of a new entrepreneurial class, a cause he considers true but partial since the Liberal-conservative conflicts and the resistance of the provinces to the capital's centralization are still visible there. However, he sees a cultural problem as central: "The social revolutionary sectors were representative of a modern worldview that transcends mere economic behavior antagonistic to the old governing oligarchy of Santiago and Concepcion, which were closely linked to Catholicism and its values and traditional social hierarchy.

Equality, most of whose members were manual workers, the new Radicalism contained very few of them and at the time of its formalization as a political party, in the 1880s, it consisted almost entirely of the provincial middle classes and the intellectual and professional element from the secondary schools and the university. "Its ideal was the emancipation of the spirit at every level: religious, social and moral" (Gazmuri: 146).

Until the formal establishment of their party, the Radicals operated through (electoral) assemblies, which were revived at election times and also maintained continuity and identification with its members and their principles and ideals, and hence it can be said that Radicalism existed as a political force from 1863–64 onward.

THE RADICAL CLUBS

The so-called Radical clubs formed a new kind of social pattern that widened the radius of Radical action beyond the strictly political or at least beyond electoral activity. The clubs grew as a result of the assemblies, and in the same cities and neighborhoods: "Not only was the 'club' a much wider social arena than the assembly; cultural activities took place there, people talked about different topics, ate and drank, and apparently gambled in moderation." Since these clubs were examples of informal social structures, they were also important vehicles for the dissemination of doctrine and Radical "culture." In contrast to 'assemblies,' the clubs had a continuity independent of electoral activity, and even though they were not structured within a formal network, "they constituted an informal network as powerful as a formal organization" (Gazmuri: 148).

Other New Forms of Non-political Sociability

By the mid-nineteenth century there appeared a type of person primarily in middle-class circles and part of the traditional

oligarchy, more precisely within males of the provincial bourgeoisie, often foreign-born, who were prospering and who in
some instances had become rich through mining and trade.
Such individuals represented a culture better expressed in non-
political sociability than in its parallel political expression. It
was a secular and rationalist culture, open to the idea that the
state should play a regulatory role in economic and social
life; nationalist, with philanthropic tendencies, critical of the
Catholic church and dogmatic morality; republican and democratic and against all rank acquired through birth, and also relatively open to the social preoccupations of the underdog. Such a
figure was vehemently anti-traditionalist and a supporter of all
progress; an admirer of European culture, concerned about education and the struggle against "obscurantism." Those identi-
fying with this culture, Radicals or members of the Reform
Club, founded new non-political forms of sociability, through
Freemasonry or the groups of volunteer firemen (Gazmuri: 170).

Freemasonry

The first Masonic lodges arose in Valparaiso, where several
foreign groups had their business and were influential, thereby
helping to spread ideas from Europe. These were already expressed in the previously mentioned political formations and
now they became visible in these new social groups that were
nonpolitical in character but very similar in their ideals of tolerance, justice, moderation, and their inclination to education
and culture.

This is how the first Chilean Masonic lodge, *L'Étoile du
Pacifique,* was founded in Valparaiso in 1850 by a group of
Frenchmen and was affiliated to the European headquarters,
the French Great Orient. A Frenchman proposed the idea in
July 1850 during an exuberant celebration of Bastille Day, and
it was taken up with enthusiasm. A year later the second lodge,
Bethesda, appeared, also in Valparaiso, this time as an adjunct
to the Massachusetts Great Lodge. Two years later properly

Chilean Masons began to be organized in Valparaiso, with the founding of the Fraternal Union Lodge, also connected to the French Great Orient. In 1862 the Great Lodge of Chile was established in Santiago and one year later there appeared Progress, Order and Liberty, and Aurora of Chile, in Valparaiso, Copiapó, and Concepción, respectively, all connected with the French Great Orient. In 1870 the Supreme Masonic Council was established in Valparaiso and by 1900 there were more than fifty Masonic lodges throughout Chile (Vial, 1981, vol. 1: 65–71).

In Chile it was social sectors of the new middle class, mainly from the provinces, that became part of this male nonpolitical form of sociability. "Santiago, the capital, fortress of traditional oligarchy," says Cristián Gazmuri, "incorporated this new form of sociability relatively late, and it took hold primarily among people who did not belong to the best-known families," with some exceptions (Gazmuri, 1991: 183). He emphasizes that what distinguishes masonry from political forms of sociability is its intellectual concern—or more precisely, a spiritual concern of a gnostic type. Despite their hermetic tendencies, Masons became defenders of rationalism and later of positivism, "insofar as they were currents opposed to the 'medieval fog' in which the Catholic Church operated. In political terms, they opted decisively for a republican democratic ideal, not only as forms of state and government, but also as civic culture broadly conceived" (ibid.: 184). One can easily imagine the size and importance of the network to which a member of the Freemasons was connected. It was constructed as a lay "brotherhood" involving tacit duties of mutual aid and solidarity amongst its members. Many foreigners became members, as a defense against the persecution aimed at them by officials of the Catholic Church, which denied them the right to be married or buried according to their own religious convictions. It is likewise easy to imagine the political scope of the Masonic institution and what it meant to be a "brother." In making contacts and obtaining aid in general they could rely on the

Masonic network throughout the country and even outside of it, says Gazmuri, adding that it was "as helpful as, if not more helpful, than a formal political connection, such as membership in a party, which in fact generally went along with it. Some Masons were Liberals, and later, in the twentieth century, some were Socialists, but the great majority were Radicals" (ibid.: 185). The historian Gonzalo Vial observes that for the emerging young liberal professionals, the Masonic lodges represented the "family" that could help them to secure their position in the world of work, analogous to the oligarchical family, whose sons secured their social position through family connections (Vial, 1981, vol. 2: 135).

Because of these features, Freemasonry acquired considerable public weight, which lasted into the mid-twentieth century. By the late nineteenth century, it had a strong presence within the teaching staff of the University of Chile, and later in the army and the country's educational system. Teachers trained at the Pedagogical Institute of the University of Chile, where Masonry was strong, were transformed, by their republican and rationalist culture, into the "the backbone that would form the generation that governed 'bourgeois Chile' from 1925 until the 1950s" (Gazmuri, 1991: 185).

Fire Fighters

As was the case with Freemasonry, the first body of fire fighters in Chile was established in Valparaiso in 1851 and was the idea of foreign residents. In 1854, the first genuine Chilean company of volunteer fire fighters was formed. An attempt in 1857 to create a similar group in Santiago was unsuccessful, and it was not until 1863 that a group was formed. The character of "politically advanced sociability" that was theirs or was attributed to them initially made the government afraid that their social function would be more than firefighting "and would transform itself (as indeed happened) into an area of free association and the formation of Liberal public opinion," and hence President Montt prohibited it (Gazmuri: 190). From the outset, the bodies of fire fighters were formed in small groups where males of the bourgeoisie could gather and where contacts and solidarity were created. Besides, according to Gazmuri, "it seems that the 'volunteers,' of upper or middle bourgeois origins, were often not just leading a life of leisure. It can be said that a good part of their social life took place around the 'Pump'" (ibid.). The "Pump" had the same meaning for fire fighters from a lower social class, the auxiliaries. Later, when the distinction between the auxiliaries and fire fighters disappeared, belonging to the same Pump or company represented a situation where all the members came together.

These two situations of sociability that we have seen, separate from politics and the obvious connections such as family, student, or professional life, are so connected to the Radical movement that the expression "Radical, fireman and Mason" is still used to define a kind of culture that is associated with practices of solidarity, mutual support, and friendliness that truly defines the Radical person, together with other cultural aspects that we shall discuss later. Both are limited to a kind of sociability practiced only by males or reserved purely for them, and, that like Radicalism itself, arose in provincial intellectual circles.

As already mentioned, in the closing decades of the nineteenth century, laicism controled secondary and university education, which was established in the 1840s by the state. Subsequently, first the Liberals, then their offspring, the Radicals, struggled to control education. In the state-supported National Institute all of the professors were secular. Many students came there from the provinces, and thus the church lost a portion of the most well-educated social sector. The first generation of students in the National Institute included Valentin Letelier, Nicolas Palacios, and Barros Borgono, nephew of Barros Arana (the generation born in the 1850s). The next generation (born around 1875) which studied in another state-supported school, the National Internado (boarding school, now the Barros Arana), also produced an intellectual political group that already belonged to the Radical Party (Vial, 1981, vol. 2, 66–103). Vial observes, "the cases in point (Letelier, Palacios, Duble, Loyola . . .) were all children of the provinces who came to the Institute as adolescents. They were all from families that were religious but had economic or family problems; they came from provincial schools run by Masons or non-religious persons. "Rationalism was imbibed . . . from the very atmosphere" (ibid.: 105). The teachers, continues Vial, converted the students to Radicalism and many in the state schools joined the youth sections of the party. These converts to secularism were the foundation of party commitment. This phenomenon of the loss of Catholic faith and its loss of strength in a portion of the aristocracy was complete by the early twentieth century and "went trickling down, passing through the successive layers to the bottom of the social pyramid" (ibid.: 105–8).

We should point out that during these decades a significant middle class was developing, particularly in the north with the Pacific War, the commercialization of nitrate, and so forth. The Chilean middle class arose with the appearance of groups of merchants, small manufacturers, and public and private office workers. Their first official entrance onto the political scene came with the election of President Arturo Alessandri in 1920 (Edwards and Frei, 1949: 227–77; Góngora, 1981: 60–61; Tironi, 1985). Frei points out that the Radical Party, which was laicist and closely linked with Freemasonry, was the interpreter of the new middle class already appearing at the end of the last century and that acquired personality in the first quarter of the twentieth century, reaching its peak by the middle of this century. Its structures, its strength, and its leaders had all come from the middle class, and through the party that class came into government administration, and exerted influence on the state apparatus, the university and the secondary schools. Nevertheless, since it was not strong enough to reach state power by itself, it drew on support from the proletariat and its parties on the three occasions that it won the presidency. By occupying the political center, it served as an intermediary between the two extreme forces (the economic right and the proletariat) and at the same time it served as a balance scale pointer, moving from one side to the other, determining who would win (Edwards and Frei, 1949: 228–29; also Moulian and Torres, 1990). It may have been just this ability to decide that caused its decline, because it caused many internal splits, some of which led to the formation of new parties which then united with the right or the left.

With the expansion of state lay education introduced by the Liberals, the Radical Party gradually became a middle-class party with its slogan "the teaching state." While the University of Chile was created in 1842 (long before the Radical Party was formed) along with the laws which entrusted public education to the state, Radicalism took root there and throughout the whole educational sector for decades, not only by keeping non-Radicals from becoming teachers, but also because they had the best teachers (Vial, 1981, vol. 2: 136). Several major figures arose from the educational arena and these later struggled to establish teacher-training schools (*escuelas normales*), preparatory schools, nursery schools, schools for the education of women, and so forth. Foreign teachers brought in made an important contribution to university formation, particularly in the field of pedagogy. "Education was political because through it the Teaching State (*El Estado Docente*)—and in the future the Teaching University (La Universidad Docente)—created a new morality and worldview provided by science" (Vial.: 151). Battles were waged over education (laicism versus Catholicism). The Catholic University was established in 1888 (see Serrano, 1994) and more Catholic schools were set up providing the setting for new social networks that eventually issued in new political parties, such as the Christian Democratic Party, the counterpart to the Radical Party in this study.

The notion of the "Teaching State" came to fullest expression in the first Radical government, with the triumph of Pedro Aguirre Cerda in 1938. Although he had been opposed to the formation of a left-wing coalition (the Popular Front), Aguirre

Cerda was nominated party candidate for the presidency and was elected president. A teacher himself, he took as his slogan "To govern is to educate." During his government, important changes took place in Chile, and with the creation of CORFO (Corporation for Development), a major step toward the country's industrialization was taken. With this move and the social mobility derived from the increased attention to public education, the middle class was at its peak, thereby helping to elect two Radical presidents after the death of Pedro Aguirre Cerda: Juan Antonio Rios and Gabriel Gonzalez Videla. Gonzalez Videla became president in 1946, as part of a coalition that included the Communist Party and all the left-wing forces.

THE FORMAL STRUCTURE OF THE RADICAL PARTY

The Radical Party is organized territorially in the form of "assemblies." These function at a district (*comuna*) level and by neighborhoods. In the recent change of statutes approved in 1995 after the merger of the Radical Party with the Social Democrat Party, the national leaders and regional organizers agreed to retain the territorial structure inherited primarily from the Radical Party. Hence, the following pyramid organization was maintained:

National headquarters
Regional councils
Communal assemblies

The highest political authority in the party is the General Council, whose voting members are the members of the parliament and thirty-eight national councillors elected to represent the thirteen regions in the country. Participating as non-voting members are the board (president, two vice-presidents, general secretary, treasurer, secretary of organization and oversight) and the president of the Supreme Tribunal.

The National Executive Committee (CEN) is composed of twenty-three representatives elected by universal vote, along with the new board.

Radical assemblies are generally considered to be the basis of internal democracy. They are open, invited and/or interested people may attend, and they are a ritual that the Radical grass-roots refuse to relinquish. "The PR," states a high official, "from its establishment in 1863 to the present day has traditionally lived around assemblies. . . . It has been greatly criticized for being a system that, in some ways, has lost its sense of modernity, that the assembly results in speech making, and so forth. But the truth is that to rid the Radical Party of the assembly would be to kill it." He revealed that during his mandate as president of the party he tried to "modernize" the party and revise its assembly-based structure. "I never could get around the assembly system," he confided, adding that he "did not want to do away with it, but rather modernize it and establish a commission system, one that would be along cell lines, non-Marxist but more executive style. Impossible! People rebelled against it. . . . So the assembly-system of assemblies, which, as you can see, is the essence of the party, says something about the reason for being a Radical. Radicals have a sense that the ongoing defense of dialogue and the defense of exchange of ideas is a fundamental value in their struggle."

FACTIONALISM AND NEGOTIATION

It is interesting to note the fact that around 1920, just as the Radical Party was reaching its peak, membership in Chilean Masonic lodges grew significantly, prompting Radicals to help, promote, and support their colleagues and to put into practice the idea of "brotherhood" learned from the Masonic lodges. Nevertheless, this brotherhood of Radicals has often broken down (at least politically). Factionalism is one of the constants within the party, and it actually seems to go hand in

hand with the concern for negotiation and reaching agreements, both between its own internal factions and with other
parties of left or right. Radicalism was barely taking its first
steps in the political arena when the first split occurred. In
1873 one of its leaders made a personal alliance with President
Errazuriz, which caused the group to reorganize (Remmer,
1984: 18). In 1887 a group of "left-wing" Radicals split off and
founded the Democratic Party to serve the interests of the
working class (ibid.: 68). Although the Radicals generally supported the idea of improving working-class conditions, most
Radical leaders regarded the workers incapable of participating
in the political arena. They considered them to be at most an
important electoral force that should be led and controlled by
the educated middle class. Another important splintering occurred as a result of the 1906 convention, where the Enrique
MacIver faction lost to Valentin Letelier. By 1919 the party
housed two currents at odds with each other: one in favor of the
working classes (socialist Radicals) and the other in favor of the
growth of the middle class (plain Radicals).

During the government of Arturo Alessandri (elected 1920)
and the subsequent Ibañez dictatorship (1927), the Radicals remained united. However, the period following the fall of Ibañez
witnessed an unprecedented reshuffling of the Chilean party
system: "in an exceptional and rapid expansion, the parties
split, and factions and new contenders arose. Never has there
been in Chilean history a comparable period of political confusion and innovation" (Drake in Scully, 1992: 121). In 1932 the
Radicals, this time in alliance with the right, once again
brought Arturo Alessandri to power, but his government, in
coalition with the Liberals and their perennial adversaries, the
Conservatives, was a brief one. In 1936 the party split again
over the repression of the railway workers during Alessandri's
presidency. The left-wing parties had begun to gain strength on
their own. The "left-wing" Radicals claimed that the party had
lost its original ideals and that its place in history was at the
side of the working masses rather than the bourgeois middle

classes (Scully, 1992: 133). The Democratic Party was established 1946, and this party supported Alfredo Duhalde against the PR's "official" candidate, Gabriel Gonzalez Videla, who won with the support of the left, including the Communist Party. Three years later the official Radical Party threw a large banquet to erase their differences with the "Democrats."

That same year, Gonzalez Videla published his Law for the Defense of Democracy, expelled the communists from the government, and began to persecute them, thereby prompting the second alliance of the Radical Party with Liberals and Conservatives. The outstanding Radical leader, Raul Rettig, today offers his opinion of this episode in terms of his party's characteristic striving for tolerance: "It was a great political error on our part to issue the Law for the Defense of Democracy, which had excesses, nothing but excesses. After all, the Communists brought some repression on themselves, but that was no justification for excluding them from acting as citizens" (R. Rettig, interview, 1995). However, this time the party did not split but "gave full support to the Gonzalez Videla government and remained united during the opposition to Ibañez" (ibid.). Gonzalez Videla was the last Radical to become president. In 1952 the alliance with the existing right was not renewed at the end of Gonzalez Videla's government and Ibañez, the former general, won the election with an overwhelming majority. With a view to the next presidential election in 1958, the decidedly right-wing Doctrinaire Radical Party, was formed in 1955. It vainly sought to make a pact with the Popular Socialists and with the People's Democracy to gain their support for the Radical candidate, Luis Bossay, in the presidential elections of that year. Bossay (and Dr. Salvador Allende) lost the elections to Jorge Alessandri Rodriguez. From then on, the RP could not recoup its losses and entered a period of sharp decline, losing the political center to the Christian Democratic Party. The Radical Party remained united during the presidency of Jorge Alessandri, a right-wing independent, and in the next election proposed Julio Duran as its candidate with the support of the right and in contention with the Socialist Salvador Allende and the Christian Democrat Eduardo Frei Montalva. Frei won, because at the last moment the right switched to him out of fear that Allende would win, and that the Radicals did not have enough votes to elect their candidate.[2]

In the 1970 election the RP formed part of the alliance that brought Salvador Allende to power. "With Allende's election the old Democratic Radical current headed by Julio Duran left the party for good" (Rettig). A little later another faction of the Radical Party abandoned Allende's government and later, during the military dictatorship, it became the Social Democrat Party. Two other main currents divided the Radical Party during this period, one led by Anselmo Sule, who like many other Radicals left Chile in exile, and the other led by Enrique Silva Cimma, who finally presided over the reunification of these two factions to become part of the alliance of opposition parties that overthrew General Pinochet in the 1988 plebiscite. In 1994 the Radical and Social Democrat parties merged, taking the name the Radical Social-Democrat Party (PRSD). In the process several leaders and activists withdrew from the party and, rather than attempting to form their own dissident party, joined the ranks of other political parties (mainly the Party for Democracy—Partido por la Democracia).

As can be deduced from this brief historical review of the factionalism in the Radical Party, this tendency, shared by all the Chilean political parties, is particularly evident in the Radical Party, perhaps because of what we have called a "vocation for tolerance," which this party regards as a badge of honor. Thus, despite some episodes of strong disagreements and internal struggles, the combatants came back together without sustaining any fatal wounds, except, as noted, in the case of Julio Duran's group. However, the party never recovered its position, and its very survival is today in question, depending on whether

2. Shortly before the election, in a complementary election in the south, a left-wing candidate won by a large majority in an episode known by the name of "Naranjazo," precipitating a sharp swerve to the right.

it gets over 5 percent of the vote in the 1996 municipal elections, the proportion it needs for its continued legal existence.[3]

OBSERVATIONS

As we have seen, the Radical Party provides a clear example of how a new class is formed, organizes itself in networks and informal groups, and eventually acquires political expression. The natural social networks created by the mining centers and incipient industrialization gradually formed their own proletarian subculture, which broke into the political arena in the 1930s when the Communist Party (with a strong international influence) emerged as a considerable electoral force (in 1937 the Communist Party won six parliamentary seats). Although the Radical Party had declared itself champion of the lowest social sectors, this relationship did not last, as these sectors created their own political representation (Communist and Socialist parties), thereby illustrating the constant Chilean tendency to horizontality. Since the 1930s there has been a multi-party system in Chile—sometimes comprising more than 29 parties—grouped into three tendencies which persist to this day: right, center, and left. Within these tendencies there can take place mergers, alliances, or negotiated agreements (Scully, 1992). These types of connections have also been established between tendencies (the center with the right and the center with the left), but never between the two extremes (Moulian and Torres, 1990: 23–28; Edwards and Frei, 1949: 242–43). An illustration of the class-based character of these three main tendencies (and, as such, of the horizontal networks) is given in the following paragraph taken from a 1949 essay written by Eduardo Frei Montalva, who points to the restructuring of the forces and parties in Arturo Alessandri's second period:

3. In the municipal elections, which took place after this study was finished, the PRSD attained almost 7 percent, and hence its prospects for the future are more hopeful than they seemed a few months previously.

In fact the differences that had fueled debates between Liberals and Conservatives for three-fourths of a century had ended. . . . They now made up a single political bloc going beyond the agreement of their leadership groups, and that came from the deep relationship that comes from representing the same economic position and the same social stratum. Both parties had the same social composition: practically all of their boards and elected representatives economically represented capital; socially, they were the old ruling class; politically, they had to defend the liberal-capitalist economic regime. . . . Both parties were destined to reach agreement because essentially nothing separated them, and hence they formed a powerful right wing bloc. (Edwards and Frei, 1949: 222).

As a corollary, we will add that in the model presented at the beginning of this work, we spoke of the two foundations on which rest the separation of the social networks that led to the formation of the political parties: the first is the social class where the network develops; the second is the ideological split over the role of religion in state affairs, already apparent at the time when only the ruling class had political expression. This sharp division over religious matters re-emerged in the twentieth century within the middle class, with the rise of the Christian Democratic Party (Coppedge, 1997).

3

Origins and Evolution of the Christian Democrat Party

The Chilean Christian Democrat Party (PDC) grew out of the National Association of Catholic Students (ANEC) and the National Falange (Falange Nacional—FN). The National Association of Students was established in Santiago in 1915 under the direction of the Jesuit Fernando Vives. In its early years this association was a center for study, not for engaging in politics. According to an informant, "Father Vives had many Christian social ideas and dedicated his life to teaching these to upper class children in the San Ignacio school. But his Jesuit superiors did not share his ideas and deported him twice—from 1913 to 1915 and from 1918 to 1931. Nevertheless, Father Fernandez Pradel continued his work," leading to the establishment of the Circles of Catholic Students for extracurricular courses. When the Jesuit Oscar Larson took charge, the ANEC became even more important among students.

Starting in the 1930s, on the advice of Cardinal Pacelli, who was then the Vatican Secretary of State and would become Pope Pius XII in 1939, the Chilean bishops wrote several pastoral letters exhorting Catholics to study and put the social teachings of Pope Leo XIII and Pope Pius XI into practice. Catholic Action programs, focusing particularly on the young Chileans, were created throughout the country (see Scully, 1992: 156–157).

Ideologically these programs were based on Pope Leo XIII's 1891 encyclical *Rerum Novarum* and on Pope Pius XI's 1928 proposals and his encyclical *Quadragesimo Anno* (1931). The "social encyclicals" analyzed the growing influence of socialist ideas in the European working class and proposed a Christian solution to their predicament. The encyclicals stated that the workers' wretched living conditions were due to the ideology of individualism and not to the economic and social structure created by ownership of land and the means of production. It was this individualistic ideology that caused the employers' hardheartedness and the greed of an uncontrolled competition. The solution lay not in class struggle or in putting the means of production under state control, but rather in collaboration between both classes in the search for the "common good" (see Scully, 1992: 156–57, also Loveman, 1988: 272–73). The Chilean students who were organized within the Catholic circles accepted these papal guidelines through pastoral or apostolic activities.

It is interesting to note how the modernizing process experienced by these young people resembles what happened in the "Chilean '48." As we saw, in 1842 there arose a group that brought together the most select members of Liberal youth in the oligarchy. Many of these young people would go on to be the most important representatives of the " '48" culture and members of the new networks that Cristián Gazmuri called "forms of sociability." In these new networks was planted the seed that grew into the new ideas and fundamental values of republican, liberal, and democratic thought. Just as would be done in the ANEC associations almost a century later, young people formed literary and artisan circles. One thing that set them apart, however, was that from the outset the young people of '48 were involved in political activities, while those in ANEC were not. From these nineteenth-century networks emerged three presidents in the second half of the century. In any case, the networks of young nineteenth-century liberals and the young twentieth-century Catholics were the breeding grounds for figures who would later play outstanding public roles in their country.

Father Oscar Larson, ANEC chaplain starting in 1927, set out to create a Catholic intellectual elite that could deal seriously with the country's social problems, while staying out of politics. This small group represented a modern vision of Catholicism based on study of the encyclicals. The basic ideas of the ANEC were derived primarily from *Rerum Novarum*, and can be summarized as follows:

1. Appreciation of the workers' situation as a social problem.
2. Recognition that the primary cause of the problem was the individualistic ideology of capitalism.
3. Reaffirmation of the right to private ownership of land and of the means of production.
4. Rejection of class struggle.
5. Advocacy of a policy of conciliation between capital and labor, with both church and state serving as arbitrators and laying down the duties of both capitalists and workers.

Among ANEC members we find such well-known names as Eduardo Frei, Bernardo Leighton, Radomiro Tomic, Jaime Eyzaguirre, Tomas Reyes, Manuel Francisco Sanchez, Clemente Perez, Alfredo Ruiz Tagle, Javier Lagarrigue, Julio Philippi, Eduardo Hamilton, Pastor Roman, Victor Delpiano, Lorenzo de la Maza, and Alejandro Silva Bascunan, from the Catholic University, and Domingo, Julio, and Jaime Santa Maria, and Fidel Aranda, from the University of Chile (Loveman, 1988: 274; Yocelevzky, 1987: 75).

The ANEC group was active between 1928 and 1931 as a student branch of Catholic Action and they devoted themselves to social work, studying ideas, and organizing other branches of Catholic Action. At the same time they took over the leadership of students at the Catholic University. In 1930 Bernardo Leighton became president of the ANEC and in 1931 he led a strike to bring down President Ibañez.[1]

1. The Catholic University of Chile was one of the main sources of social Catholicism among young people. From 1916 on, under its rector, Bishop Martin Rucker Sotomayor, it had organized Catholic Student Circles. In 1931, it contributed to promoting the spread of the Catholic Action Movement,

In 1932, one of the old leaders of the Conservative Party, Rafael Luis Gumucio, saw the need to renew the internal party cadres to shake them out of their stagnation. Although he did not share their Social-Christian ideas he thought it would be a good idea to bring in young people from ANEC to energize his party, and therefore he invited them to join the Conservative Party. After an arduous debate, a group of young men joined the ranks of the Conservative youth movement through the Assembly for Conservative Propaganda, which was connected to the party. Among them were Bernardo Leighton, Rafael Agustín Gumucio, Radomiro Tomic, Manuel Francisco Sanchez, Manuel Garretón, and Eduardo Frei.

Some of the points of agreement between the ANEC youth and the Conservatives were the recognition of papal authority, the basic principles of the Chilean constitution and of the Catholic church, particularly, advocacy of nonviolence for solving social conflicts, and the principles of law, order and hierarchy (Fleet, 1985: 45).

ANEC members had innovative ideas and, although in other aspects they clashed with the principles of the Conservatives—as, for example, in their intention to remain independent and to create a guild-type labor system—by joining the Conservative Party they became involved in national political life. Such involvement was possible because it was the only party in the national arena, inasmuch as President Ibañez had prohibited all political activities in 1927.

However, the priests who served as advisors to these circles were being told by their superiors how to act to bring the students into the Conservative Party. According to an informant who followed the process closely, "In 1937 Archbishop Jose Horacio Campillo of Santiago—a very conservative man, to be sure—called Jorge Gomez, who was then a young priest and a

---

founded in 1928 by Pope Pius XI as a reaction against the worldwide advance of communism and socialism. The ANEC was brought under this movement. See Scully, 1992: 154–61; also Yocelevzky, 1987: 130–50.

very influential ANEC advisor, and said to him, 'You know what young people are like; you have to let them fly, but you tie a string to one foot and let them fly, and when the time comes you tug the string and the young person will drop into the Conservative Party.'"

The association that the young ANEC members entered was viewed as the waiting room for the Conservative Party. Even so, the entry of these young men into the party was always problematic and was never fully achieved (see Loveman, 1988, and Fleet, 1985).

The ANEC group went on to be the expression of a process of modernization of the entire system and of the political elite within Conservative ranks. From this time on, ANEC's young people began to change their ideas about involvement in politics. The trip of Eduardo Frei and Manuel Garretón to Rome in 1933 to attend the International Congress for Catholic University Students was decisive in the development of their ideas and had an enormous influence on the ANEC, because they had the opportunity to speak with the main advocates of Social-Christian ideas, including Jacques Maritain in France. That same year the Center for Conservative Students was established and it became the center for all the activities of the Association. Although its purpose was to recruit Catholic students, enrollment in the Center did not entail implied membership in the Conservative Party. Indeed, during those months they were already attempting to define the position of the ANEC vis-à-vis the party.

In 1934, the Center began to publish the journal *Lircay*, which soon became very influential throughout the country. In 1935 its members called for a national conference to gather all the country's Catholic youth. With this in mind, in July 1935 they published a manifesto called "To Chilean Youth" presenting the idea that the country was undergoing a crisis of spiritual and material values, a crisis that would also affect every country, and that was rooted in the existence of political regimes inspired by the principles of liberal democracy which had abandoned "this spiritual principle which should be the soul of humanity in its entirety" (Yocelevzky, 1987: 81). In opposition to these liberal principles, they advocated an organic conception of society, corporately structured, organizing people according to their function. Among other things, they proposed a strong state, capable of equalizing social forces, and they affirmed their adherence to the existing legal framework as the only route to their proposed objectives.

The conference for which this manifesto was prepared took place on October 12 that year, and there the delegates agreed to form the National Conservative Youth Movement, electing Bernardo Leighton as its first president. The movement was to be committed to the Conservative Party only at the national level; the local branches would be independent of the party organization. On this point the ANEC youth leaders were supported by people in the Conservative Party and from others who had previously tried to establish a Social-Christian organization, who accordingly recognized the new movement as the primary Social-Christian organization, which people from both sides joined. Hence, for the first time the group was responsible for a youth political organization that was not student-based. The organization sought to bring together Chilean youth as a whole, and it spread nationally through those students who after graduation went (or returned) to the provinces to work, and became politically active there.

Although the movement had attempted to remain independent by remaining relatively autonomous from the Conservative Party, the path to its integration with the Chilean political elite appeared rather to lead to its becoming part of the party. This contradiction became particularly obvious in 1937 when, on the suggestion of Rafael Luis Gumucio, who was conspicuously a member of the Conservative Party, Bernardo Leighton was appointed labor minister in President Alessandri's government. That same year Eduardo Frei joined the National Executive Committee of the Conservative Party, representing the National Conservative Youth Movement, with the help of two long-time members of this committee. Previously, in March

1933, Manuel Garreton Walker, a member of the Movement, had been elected member of parliament for the Conservative Party (Yocelevzky, 1987: 83–84).

THE NATIONAL FALANGE

In 1936 the term "National Falange" began to replace that of the Movement within the Conservative Party. According to an informant, the name Falange was most certainly taken from the plainly fascist Spanish Falange: "Later they never wanted to admit where they got the name 'Falange'; I think that to our shame, it must have come from the Spanish Falange, for our sins."

The purpose in changing the name was to emphasize the independent political position that this group had always shown vis-à-vis the Conservatives and other youth factions, such as the Social-Christians. This led to a "separation without a break" within the Conservatives, at which point Manuel Garretón Walker became a candidate for congress. Six more Falange candidates for parliament were introduced into the political arena: "The Falange started with six members of parliament, two or three of whom continued. The Falange was represented in parliament from the outset, but they had been chosen by the Conservative Party, not by us," recalls the same informant.

The Falangists devoted more time to their own organizations and to social work than to assembly activities: "This child of the Conservative Party became a major opponent, and the Conservative Party could not forgive what it regarded as real treason: that these young men had violated discipline, set up shop on their own, and even worse, were promoting a line of political thinking that was in conflict with the values defended by the Conservative Party," continues the informant.

Characteristic features of the National Falange throughout this entire period were its centrist position, its small electoral support, and its strong integration into the political elite. In its

first few years, the Falange did not manage to attract wide support from the lower or middle social sectors and hence its influence on national electoral life was mainly limited to university students. That did not hold it back, however, and gradually
it adapted to the direction that historical-social development
was taking the country. Because the Chilean parliament was a
multi-party system, even though the Falange members were
represented by a small minority, that minority could still be decisive when blocs were formed. They were thus given the
chance to appear on the ballot, and even to receive ministries,
as in the case of Bernardo Leighton. We can thus see that their
leaders were given positions, a presence, and participation that
was not exactly in keeping with their electoral strength. That
they would remain in the system was thereby assured, since
the cadres thus recognized maintained a personal and geo-
graphically located electoral clientele sufficient to secure their
presence in Congress and their participation in the coalition
system (see Fleet: 85–102).

The growth of Falange influence among university students
put the movement ahead of the other parties in reaching into
the middle classes and, particularly their youngest and most
modern sectors.[2]

The break between conservatives and Falangists was not far
off. The incompatibility between reactionary political tendencies of the traditional leading group of the Conservative Party
and the young social Christians' concerns for the renewal and
modernization of the national social and political structure led
to their separation. This crucial moment occurred in the 1938
presidential elections, in which the Conservatives decided to
support Gustavo Ross, in opposition to the Falangists who favored the Radical, Pedro Aguirre Cerda. When Ross lost to the
Popular Front's Aguirre Cerda, a crisis broke out within the
Conservative Party. Walker, leader of the Conservatives, blamed
the Falangists for the failure, and so on November 29, 1938, the

2. For an analysis of the problem of the other parties, such as the Radical,
the Communist, and the Socialist, see the work of Timothy Scully (1992).

Conservative Party executive body ordered that the Falange be reorganized. This measure was rejected by the Falangists and in December the Falange became an independent political party.

The National Falange was made up of Catholic youth with grand ideals of a social, political, and economic restoration. It was part of the reformist wing of the middle classes, and hence it could not remain on the sidelines of national events. Under Frei's leadership, it supported the Radical Juan Antonio Rios in the presidential elections of 1942 and went into the government, obtaining several positions. Within the party, however, there were differing opinions about this collaboration. There were debates among those who supported the collaboration and those who criticized the government.

The first factional confrontation within the Falange occurred in 1946 at a meeting of its National Executive known as the "Barber's Congress," since this conference was organized in the barbers' union headquarters. There they discussed which candidate to support in the presidential elections of that year, whether the Radical, Gabriel Gonzalez Videla, or the right-wing Conservative candidate Dr. Eduardo Cruz-Coke, who was regarded as advocating Social-Christian ideas (Fleet: 50–51). According to informants active in party politics, the factions were the "purists," who dominated the Executive of the party and favored Cruz-Coke for his Social-Christian ideas and the "conformists" who saw that Gonzalez Videla represented popular interests. The purists were represented by Radomiro Tomic, Pedro J. Rodriguez, and Ricardo Ferrando. The conformists were Jorge Rogers, Manuel Francisco Sanchez and Bernardo Leighton, Eduardo Frei, and Rafael Gumucio. This time the purists won and announced their support for the candidature of Cruz-Coke. The defeated faction preferred not to participate in the electoral campaign.

By this time the Falange had consolidated certain positions within the political system, representing Catholic middle class university students. In 1945 they had founded a publishing house (Editorial Del Pacífico), and a theoretical journal *Política y Espíritu*. The party grew, but most of the new members came from the same social group that had started the ANEC. The second generation, those who joined as Falangists was also made up of university students. In 1948, when Gonzalez Videla's government issued the Law for the Defense of Democracy, which expelled the Communists, the Falangists decided to leave the government. In 1949 the Falangists formed an electoral alliance in opposition to Gonzalez Videla, known as the FRAS (Radical Agrarian Socialist Falange) along with Democratic Radicals, the Labor-Agrarians, and the Socialists. In the parliamentary elections of that year Eduardo Frei Montalva was elected senator for the first time. The Falange obtained 3.92 percent of the votes. In this campaign the Falangists supported the women's right to vote. It should be pointed out that the influence of the Catholic Church on women would later be a fundamental basis for Christian Democratic activity, and that from the 1940s to the 1960s, the Christian Democrats pursued electoral reforms that would stop vote buying, which was used primarily to control the peasant vote (Fleet: 98).

The Falangists returned to Gonzalez Videla's government in 1950, forming part of the so-called "cabinet of social sensitivity," with Social-Christian conservatives and radicals also participating. Leighton occupied the post of minister of education and Ignacio Palma, that of land and colonization. However, a Falangist proposal for electoral reform was blocked by right-wing opposition in parliament. The willingness of President Gonzalez Videla to negotiate reform prompted the Falange ministers to resign and the Falange to leave the administration, although the party continued to support it in parliament.

Before the 1952 presidential election, the Christian Democratic Council discussed which strategies to follow. They wanted to present a common candidate supported by the Radicals, the Social-Christian Conservatives, and the Falangists. The Falange first proposed Frei, but finally agreed to support Enrique Alfonso, a Radical. When he lost the election, the Radicals cut off all ties to the Falangists. The Christian Democrat Party began to be formed shortly afterwards. One of our informants remembers that even some Radicals were not in agreement with the choice of Alfonso to be presidential candidate, and they were so disgusted when he was not elected that they opted to leave the alliance.

After the triumph of Carlos Ibañez in the 1952 elections, there was a discussion within the Falange about the character the party should have. Some were of the opinion that the party should adapt to developments in Chilean politics, inasmuch as it was changing (the accent in party politics was shifting toward individual leaders, as it was elsewhere in Latin America), and that hence they should focus their energies on enhancing Frei's public image, since his influence on national life was gathering momentum.[3]

This position, combined with the internal factions, and the recent electoral failure, caused a great deal of confusion within the Falange, prompting several to leave. When Rafael Agustín Gumucio was elected president of the Falange in 1953, he commented that he was taking over a "bankrupt" organization (Fleet: 101).

CHRISTIAN DEMOCRACY

The Christian Democrat Party (PDC) was founded in 1957 as a result of the merger of the National Falange with the Social-Christian Conservative Party and some former Ibañez supporters. Those in the Ibañez group joined the PDC either as individuals who supported Eduardo Frei's presidential candidature in 1958, or as part of organizations that merged with the new party: e.g., the Agrarian Labor Party and the Popular National Party (Yocelevzky, 1984).

Within these groups we can point out those of the Social-Christian Conservative sector, such as Horacio Walker, Jorge Mardones, and Eduardo Cruz-Coke (who stood in sharp rivalry to Eduardo Frei, and who accordingly did not play a very direct

---

3. This group was identified by Rafael Agustín Gumucio as "people who were united around the Editorial del Pacifico press," (Yocelevzky, 1987, 101).

role in the party or last long in it). Another group was made up of what was left of the Ibañez followers, including Jorge Lavanderos, Jose Musalem, and Mario Hamuy. An informant recalls that there were others, like Alejandro Hales, who was one of Frei's government ministers, but never joined the party.

Almost all of them were center-right. The new party and its leader, Eduardo Frei, very soon achieved a certain presence and prestige in political and social life, and hence Frei obtained 20.69 percent of the votes in the 1958 presidential election. This small victory launched Frei and his party on their way toward playing a major role in the Chilean political process.

It is interesting to note that, within the PDC, the different groups soon dissolved. The Social-Christian group, for example, fit in quickly, perhaps because it was composed of the same social network, their ideologies were similar, their origins were the same, and they had helped organize the party. The Ibañez group always retained certain characteristics of its own, a certain uniqueness: most of its members came from an agrarian background in the south, and always kept their separate network. According to an informant, it was for ideological reasons that different tendencies later emerged.

The PDC was rooted in the middle strata of society, and although by 1958 it appeared as a hegemonic force within them, it also came to represent a political expression of these sectors starting at that same time, as is obvious in its ideology. The Falangists provided the new party not only with a leader (Frei) but also a formulator of ideology (Jaime Castillo Velasco) and its ideological foundations, such as the claim to have its "own path" and "nonviolence." The rise of a new party with these characteristics reflected the need to modernize Chilean political life that began after the fall of the Ibañez dictatorship in 1931.[4]

The 1950s and the 1960s were marked by what was being called "modernization" and "development" (begun in the '40s)

---

4. For a characterization of the Ibañez movement, consult Stallings (1978) and Urzua (1986).

which in practice meant moving from a traditional agricultural society to a modern industrial one, with all the social implications entailed. At this point Narciso Irureta was the president of the party. Frei had a much broader political center and he was selected as candidate for the 1958 presidential elections, producing the results noted above. A congress held in 1959 was significant in terms of the ideological process within the PCD, and particularly as expressed in three speeches given. One of them presented the view of those, including Jaime Castillo, who advocated a vanguard party. A second speech, reflecting the views of Rafael Agustín Gumucio, Julio Silva Solar and Alberto Jerez, took the opposite point of view, that is, that the party should ally itself with the left; this group later chose to split from the party. The third group argued for broadening the party and its suggestions combined the two previous theses. In this group were Frei, Aylwin, and several others (informant from that time; see also Scully, 1992: 196).

The ideas of ECLA (Economic Commission for Latin America) began to be influential within the Christian Democrats. Combining the developmental vision of the ECLA theories with those of the Jesuit Roger Vekemans on social promotion, the Christian Democrats articulated a Christian-inspired formula as a solution to Chile's problems. In keeping with this proposal, Christian Democrat leaders spoke not of class struggle but rather of "marginalized" sectors who were to be "integrated" into society. These ideas drew large portions of the urban poor to the party.

It was not only the urban poor who were drawn into the PDC, which began to work with peasants in the early 1960s, and surprisingly, it succeeded in organizing the peasantry. Undertaking these previously forbidden actions, however, meant confronting a thorny problem: mobilizing the peasants and winning their loyalty from the landed gentry. This, later compounded with Frei's agrarian reform (1967), caused the landowners to respond by moving further to the right and by categorically rejecting the PDC's agrarian policy. Starting in the 1960s, every party was competing for the peasant vote. The

Christian Democrats invited the tenant farmers to join the Movement for Peasant Liberation that they had created.

THE FREI ADMINISTRATION 1964–1970

Eduardo Frei won the presidency under the slogan "Revolution in Liberty," put forward as an alternative to the revolution suggested by Marxists, which, according to the PDC, implied violence, loss of property, and loss of liberty. The revolution in liberty was the PDC response to the dilemmas of industrial society, recognizing implicitly and explicitly the need for fundamental change, even a revolutionary one, to overcome Chile's terrible social inequalities. Thus, the party gave a political shape to the teachings of the Catholic church expressed in the social encyclicals mentioned earlier. In addition, after World War II, the Holy See, worried by the advance of Marxism in Chile, gave a new impetus and support to Catholic organizations of workers, students, women, and peasants. That was when the Falange emerged as an alternative for reformers, technicians, and professional people to confront the conservative rigidity of the traditional parties and the opportunism of the Radicals, enabling it to win prestige and presence, by promoting major reforms based on the church's social doctrine (Loveman, 1988: 275).

The activity of young Catholics that gave rise to the PDC had made notable advances in organizing the peasants, which in its turn was to give greater credibility to its principles. In the 1950s Emilio Lorenzini organized the Christian Land Federation, which later became part of the Chilean Union Action. (ASICH). This organization, started by a Jesuit priest with special permission from the head of the Jesuits and Pope Pius XII, produced, according to historian Brian Loveman, "a thorn in the side of both the Marxists and of the traditional parties in Chile." In the same period, the Belgian Jesuit Roger Vekemans arrived in Chile, sent there by the Jesuit general to help the church in its struggle against Marxism. This social scientist founded the Centro Bellarmino in Chile, a research center and a precursor of future non-governmental organizations (NGOs), which became the spearhead of anti-communism in Chile in the next decade, and from which Vekemans waged an intellectual, organizational, and political campaign under the umbrella of DESAL (Center of Social Development for Latin America). Alongside its research work, DESAL promoted the formation of organizations of neighborhoods, women, unions, agricultural committees, discussion groups, and semi-political groups that were to play a major role in the 1964 presidential campaign. Meanwhile, in 1960, ASICH created the Union of Christian Peasants and at the same time Rural Catholic Action and the Institute of Rural Education (IER) gave rise to the National Association of Peasant Organizations. (ANOC) After being trained in the IER, leaders became paid officials of the Institute at the same time as they provided leadership in rural labor disputes, created Christian-oriented rural organizations, and combated communism in the countryside (Loveman, 1988: 278).

Hence, the word "revolution" in Frei's campaign slogan was more than mere rhetoric; in fact all of this mobilization of the peasantry took on its own momentum that later proved to be difficult to manage or manipulate. With the government of Jorge Alessandri (1958–64) weakened, the PDC, linked to the growing Catholic peasant league movement, emerged as a significant alternative to the left-wing coalition, the Popular Action Front (FRAP). The most important Christian Democrat leaders, including Eduardo Frei, had been schoolmates of the major figures working at Vekemans' Centro Bellarmino. Thus, "personal ties reinforced the doctrinal and ideological convictions among the PDC and the Jesuit intellectuals," (ibid.: 279), including Father Renato Poblete, who is still director of the "Hogar de Cristo" [Home of Christ].

Once Frei took office in 1964, the faction that put forward the idea that "they could govern by themselves" became increasingly powerful within the party. Paradoxically, the very things that the party had done to widen its electoral base began to generate new conflicts which forced it towards the center. By attracting not only the "marginal population" but also unionized urban workers, the PDC had invaded left-wing territory, and by organizing peasants it had touched the most sensitive and dangerous nerves of the landowners, who, far from being divided, formed a solid front with the Conservatives and the Radicals.[5]

All these factors, combined with the range and gravity of the social and economic problems in Chile, the lack of funds to implement the government program, and the opposition which the right- and left-wing parliament members could still exercise in congress, meant that the deep and ambitious reforms promised by Frei were largely unworkable. Almost all the aspects of the government program threatened either the traditional elite or the influence of the left-wing on the popular classes (Loveman: 280). By holding up the "Revolution in Liberty" as a positive alternative to the Cuban model, U.S. policymakers sought to bolster the Christian Democrats and support American interests in Chile. However, this policy ensnared the Christian Democrat administration in the nets of American foreign policy, including the Vietnam War, and exacerbated the internal divisions in the government party, since the PDC Youth and the more populistic elements in the party refused to be identified with foreign capital, imperialism, the U.S. embassy, and the Vietnam War. The upshot was the departure from the party of a significant group of young leaders who were linked socially and in ideas, and who set up on their own by founding the MAPU (Movement of Popular and Unitarian Action) party. Moreover, even though Frei could not fully carry out the objectives of his reform program, his government mobilized thousands of women, workers, peasants, and students who adopted various organizational forms dependent on the stimulus or subsidies of the government, and who came to expect permanent economic benefits or the extension of governmental services. "The distribution of consumer goods, of agricultural materials and work through political agencies such

5. For greater details on this process, see Scully (1992).

as the Popular Promotion and the Institute for Agricultural Development (INDAP) created a vast network of patronage and sinecures that linked bureaucrats, party leaders, workers, and peasants to government funds" (Loveman: 284).

This first PDC government that attempted to put the church's social doctrine into practice, did not manage to reconcile the interests of capitalists with those of the dispossessed. By mobilizing and promoting the popular class, stimulating its wish for action ("raising its consciousness"), it actually made it more difficult to achieve such macroeconomic objectives as lower inflation, greater production, and more internal savings and investment, and hence the PDC ultimately lost the majority support that its proposals had aroused six years before.

THE PDC AND THE ALLENDE GOVERNMENT

According to Michael Fleet, a student of the Christian Democrat movement, the conflict between this party and the left was the "product of a lack of confidence and mutual hostility" (Fleet, 1985: 124). If one adds the already observed strong tendency toward isolation and following "its own path," one can understand the relation between the PDC and the Popular Unity government was destined to end in an irresolvable confrontation. Even during the Frei government, these political forces had few contacts. The Socialists were contemptuous of the PDC political project, while the Communists seemed to be more interested in attracting progressive sympathizers than in collaborating with the government. Within the PDC, although some activists were in favor of discussions and proposed other initiatives, they never had the support of the party, the government, or Frei himself. Neither Frei nor most Christian Democrat activists had the slightest interest in working with the labor organizations or with the Marxist parties, since "to do so would be the equivalent of accepting that the left was something real with which one had to coexist and enter into commitments, and this was not a concession that they were willing to make, either ideologically nor politically" (ibid.: 145).

The sociologist and political analyst Manuel Antonio Garretón (*El Mercurio*, November 12, 1993) believes that what rendered the Popular Unity's political project impossible lay in its intention to produce a revolution by non–revolutionary and democratic means, without having the constitutional majority to do so. "And in Chile," he notes, "historically a majority is constructed not by an overwhelming electoral majority, but by agreement between parties. Without such agreement, any proposal for significant change is condemned to failure." He believes that the main lesson from this period is the need for a strategy for building a majority. It was "not only the Popular Unity that was to blame" for the lack of such a strategy; "on this score Christian Democracy also has to settle accounts with its past."

All-out opposition to the Allende government was not obvious at first. Fleet outlines three phases of its development: constructive opposition, constitutional opposition (struggling against the government at an institutional and mass level), and a final period that began with the parliamentary elections in March, 1973, where the PDC began to tilt toward solution outside the law. The deterioration in the relationship was so fast and drastic as to indicate a strong resistance within the PDC to accepting a progressive project different from their own and to relinquishing its calling to hegemony. A strong "we-ness" is in evidence here, one proper to a strongly developed subculture. Garretón and Moulian, quoted by Fleet, see the PDC opposition to Allende as an effort to keep its identity and electoral support intact (Garretón and Moulian, 1979:188). Nevertheless, different currents within the PDC also came to the fore during this period. Fleet identifies three of these: leftists, Frei supporters, and well-known figures in the party who, without considering themselves a group, were united by common identifiable characteristics: they did in fact constitute what we have called a network. The first came from the rebel group, part of which had left the party in 1969, and founded the MAPU party during the

Frei government. Their main support came from the Christian Democrat university students, although they also had the sympathies of workers, women, peasants, and young technical workers. During the Frei administration, this group—which also ultimately left the party to form one of its own, *"La Izquierda Cristiana"* (Christian Left)—advocated an alliance with the left, which they urged starting with the 1970 presidential candidacy of Radomiro Tomic's, in which they played an important role and imparted an anti-right emphasis to the campaign.

The second, pro-Frei, group (which had official status when he was in office) reflected another network composed primarily of former Frei administration officials: ministers, members of parliament, and provincial and communal leaders. Although Frei had already left the presidency, these former colleagues of his shared his anti-Marxist, "developmentalist" position, and were resolved to continue as the "progressive" alternative to the Marxist revolution, hoping to once more arouse the support of the right for their project, as had happened in 1964.

The third group included, as we have already mentioned, outstanding PDC figures, such as Radomiro Tomic himself, Bernardo Leighton, Renan Fuentealba, Benjamin Prado, and Narciso Irureta. Fleet characterizes these as "social democrats," defenders of civic liberties and moderately anti-capitalist in their social and economic views: "always looking for a painless non-coercive reform of the social structures." According to Fleet, these divisions within the party were more rooted in politics than in the class system. Fleet, however, proposes to extend or refine certain points in the arguments of Garretón and Moulian, particularly those with regard to the class composition of the PDC (these authors see it as complex and contradictory, emphasizing the multiclass system of its adherents—workers, middle class, modernizing bourgeois—and argue that each one of these sectors influenced the party at a particular time); its initial stance vis-à-vis the Allende administration; developments in popular support aroused by the Allende government; and relationships between its leaders, activists and followers or sympathizers in general. To analyze the PDC during the Popular Unity government, Fleet presents five proposals to be explored:

- that the working-class basis of the party in fact expanded, but over time it became progressively more anti-UP and anti-Allende;
- that the hostility of the PDC towards Allende and the parties supporting him was primarily political in its origin and basic character;
- that the dominating force of the PDC party continued to be petit bourgeois, whose class interests were predominantly social and political;
- that the working class base of the party supported but did not at all press for the shift to the right that occurred in the party in the years 1972 and 1973;
- that the social breakdown and trauma of the last six months of the Allende government were so deep and widespread that they would affect political convictions and sentiments for years to come (Fleet, 1985: 131).

In highlighting the role played by the political aspect in the confrontation of the PDC with the Popular Unity government, and stressing the interaction between factors of class and politics, Fleet seeks to refute the argument that the bourgeois condition of the DC—and its opposition to any change in favor of the working classes—was the reason for the increasingly categorical rejection of the Allende government. The political aspect of its opposition, namely its need to set itself apart as a sui generis political force with its own characteristics, had the effect of reinforcing the PDC's "self" vis-à-vis the "other-ness" of its main adversary during this period. The issue was not one or another social or economic measure adopted by the UP government, but rather that of resisting the other-ness toward which it felt an overwhelming lack of trust. In Fleet's words: "For some, it did not matter what the other parties or Allende did, 'trusting them was inconceivable.'"

THE PDC DURING THE MILITARY DICTATORSHIP

With regard to the period of military government, the informants agreed in a general assessment that there were three sharp profiles: the Christian Democrats interviewed hold that the party firmly opposed the regime, suffered political persecution, and made efforts to maintain a minimum of political activity, fundamentally through social or societal activities, largely under the protection of the Catholic Church. Politically, the Christian Democrat position was first expressed publicly in the 1980 plebiscite, where the main PDC leader at that time, Eduardo Frei Montalva, headed an active campaign for a "No" vote, against the constitution submitted in the plebiscite, and against the route to the future designed by the military junta; that is, by voting "Yes," one was approving the new constitution and the presidential mandate of General Pinochet would be extended for another eight years.

Whatever expectations the PDC might have had of exercising some influence on the military regime or of becoming a means for restoring democracy were quickly cut short. Because the military junta from the outset regarded its government as foundational in nature, there was no room in it for the "honored politicians" or for politics as practiced in Chile up to September 11, 1973. Thus, although some well-known Christian Democrats were invited to perform some government functions, primarily in technical posts, the party soon had to realize that its collaboration was not sought for helping with either programs or leadership. The party position moreover, was to offer or accept technical collaboration, not political commitment to the new regime. The PDC Balmaceda radio network was censored and closed several times, along with the newspaper *La Prensa,* which stopped publication in February 1974, supposedly because of "financial problems." This lack of financial resources was primarily due to the fact that the government stopped placing paid announcements in the paper and thus cut off an important source of income. At the same time, its criticism of the junta's economic policy and its careful reservations about human rights violations were ignored. Lacking resources and a public platform for presenting or pressing its positions, the PDC continued to lose influence, and by late 1974 it was already adopting a position of open criticism. So the PDC accepted that its initial strategy towards the military regime (critical collaboration) had failed and it joined the opposition.

From the outset, nevertheless, the stances of Christian Democrats towards the military coup and later towards the new regime exhibited at least three tendencies at the leadership level: one hailed the coup as salvation from an unacceptable political situation, by ending the "Chilean Way to socialism"; a second recognized that the situation in the country had become unsustainable and accordingly accepted the coup; a third tendency viewed the "solution" with apprehension and guilt feelings (Fleet: 179–80). As already noted, the sequence of events gradually erased the boundary lines between these positions, and they converged on the need for criticism and opposition. That did not mean, however, there was a single position on what was to be done because, despite everything, many followers of Christian Democracy were in favor of the junta and were willing to collaborate. Hence, even though it was decided that collaborators should be punished, most chose not to work with the left-wing forces, and only a minority did so. At a general party council in April 1975, the majority (68.2 percent) approved a line of "critical active independence" while only 9.1 percent advocated open opposition. A significant 28.8 percent was in favor of a critical collaboration and 4.6 percent in favor of full collaboration (ibid.: 181). In short, at this assembly the PDC agreed to a line of active opposition, without joining the left-wing opposition, which was pressuring for the formation of an anti-fascist front. Hence, the Christian Democrat leaders Bernardo Leighton and Renan Fuentealba were bitterly criticized by some fellow party members further to their right for having met in Caracas with leaders of the Socialist, Radical, and Christian Left parties, and for supporting the idea of a united center-left opposition. At this time, a key PDC figure,

Eduardo Frei, broke his many months of silence in mid-1975, and besides giving a long interview to a national magazine (*Ercilla*), later in December published an essay titled "The Mandate of History," in which he first attacked the military junta for its economic and human rights policies.

This stance was taken during the deepening economic recession suffered by the country as a result of the economic "shock policy," which, however, had a greater impact on union mobilization than on party activity. Inasmuch as that union activity went into abeyance after the military coup, it is worth mentioning that the Christian Democrats managed to reach leading positions in the country's important unions. As Fleet points out, these leaders—all of them anti-left—defended the regime for eighteen months, but in 1975 they formed the "Group of Ten," under the auspices of the governmental Office for Coordination of Trades, and began to go to work against political firings and low salaries. The junta responded with indifference to their arguments that the government's attitude to the labor sector and its leaders discredited those who wanted to collaborate and favored the left, and it refused to set a precedent by negotiating with its critics (Fleet: 186–87). The upshot was a gradual increase in worker protests in 1977–78, even though demonstrations and strikes were still prohibited. The PDC even participated in the May 1 celebrations of those years alongside the Socialist and Communist parties. The response of the regime was greater repression and persecution of Christian Democrat union leaders, which frightened some but spurred many to struggle more energetically for workers' rights. It could be said that to some extent the grassroots went further than their leaders. As Fleet says, the leaders "were dragged along by increasingly impatient members and by the authoritarian and insensitive response of the government authorities. Under these circumstances, the need and desire for a greater solidarity among the union groups obliged them to forget their antipathies and ideological fears" (ibid.: 187). The effect of this union mobilization was to break up the Group of Ten. Four of the federations within it withdrew into a softer position, while another three formed the National Coordination of Unions, together with the Communists, Socialists and other left-wing groups. Its first national leader was the Christian Democrat, Manuel Bustos, who showed a great presence of spirit and bravery in his role as union leader. He was strongly attacked and persecuted, imprisoned, suffered the pains of exile, and when the Sole Worker Federation was re-formed, he was elected as its first president, a post which he held throughout the government of President Aylwin and part of that of Eduardo Frei Ruiz-Tagle, until 1996.

This "need and desire for greater solidarity among the union groups" finally began to break through the wall of the PDC's mistrust in the Marxist left, at least among unions. Bustos and other young leaders crossed the line separating them and began to act in coordination with the other opposition forces. The Communists had also abandoned the idea of making an alliance only with the most progressive part of the PDC and sought an agreement with all sectors of the party.

The other area where forces opposing the dictatorship were to be found was in the defense of human rights, and more specifically in aiding and supporting victims of violations of these rights. This activity was developed mainly under the auspices of the Catholic Church and its institutions, initially in the Pro-Peace Committee, and subsequently in the Vicariate of Solidarity, which were ecumenical organizations in which PDC, Radical and left-wing activists were involved. Also, according to the Christian Democrat informants, party activists became involved on other levels, such as student, professional associations, sports activities, and neighborhood social activities. It should be recalled that the PDC was in recess starting with the military coup of 1973 (its formal dissolution did not occur until 1977), and hence it was difficult to have presence as a political party. In addition, its refusal to participate in a left-wing anti-dictatorship alliance and the predominance of leaders who backed a center-right solution led the PDC to favor seeking to come together with forces of the democratic right and even with so-called "soft" sectors within the military government itself, an option with little likelihood of success. In Fleet's analysis, this was because over time the PDC's potential allies in the military field tended to disappear through death, retirement, or dismissal. Finally, weakened as it was, "The party had increasingly less to offer its 'friends' in the moderate right." Moreover, as Fleet points out, the right in Chile always showed a certain mistrust of the PDC and not only towards its most leftist sectors but also to the moderates. In their eyes, these sectors "although they were more sympathetic were still too full of their ideology and too little appreciative of other political forces" (ibid.: 192). The PDC finally realized that the conditions for alliance with the "democratic" or "moderate" right did not exist. It was recognized that democracy would have to be won back in other ways, especially when in the late 1970s the country began to experience a kind of economic boom with the arrival of enormous amounts of foreign capital. Although this boom gave the military government a momentary triumph, it also undermined it through the catastrophe of world recession and the foreign debt crisis, in the early 1980s. In any case, at the General Council of the PDC in April 1980, the analysis of the party's situation showed a very negative balance: low organizational level, little grassroots activity, and almost non-existent mass support. The information gathered revealed that the military government still enjoyed considerable support within the PDC ranks, even when compared with President Allende's period. This negative information forced the PDC to look for ways of vitalizing the party and finding cooperation with other democratic groups, including the left-wing, following the example of the labor unions.

As the September 1980 plebiscite on the 1980 Constitution approached, Eduardo Frei Montalva headed up the "No" movement, and engaged in energetic political activity along with other opposition forces. As we know, the "Yes" option triumphed and, according to various analysts, this showed the organizational and political strength of Pinochet's government, possible fraudulent and intimidating actions against the voters notwithstanding. The left-wing opposition and the PDC agreed: the dictatorship emerged even stronger from this vote. But they did not agree over how to confront the situation. The PDC tended toward a position of political realism: that change could not be expected in the short run, that a patient and detailed grassroots action of infiltration was needed in universities and industries, in neighborhoods and military barracks, working patiently to renew and invigorate party doctrine and organization. The left-wing opposition, by contrast, arguing that moderate and discreet opposition had failed, opted for stronger resistance, although the different tendencies and parties each gave a different meaning to the notion of force. (It was just at this time that the Communist Party raised the banner of "all forms of struggle.")

With the economic collapse in the early 1980s, the military government entered its final stage. The catastrophic situation faced by industries, financial companies, banks, executives on all levels, salaried workers, employees, and others brought about what the forcibly imposed antidemocratic measures, and the repression and the privation of liberty could not; i.e. it generated the courage to protest. Thus began the era of popular protest, the mobilization of many citizens and, in tandem with it, consultations between different opposition forces. They finally agreed to participate in the 1988 plebiscite ("No" to General Pinochet remaining in power), calling all Chileans to register in the electoral rolls. The PDC completed the process of registering of its party as the Party for Democracy, an "instrumental" party, one with no doctrine or ideological grip, brought to life in order to have representatives at the voting tables to defend the "No" vote. The victory of the "No" marked the most important point in the process which culminated when the Christian Democrat, Patricio Aylwin, a supporter of the Parties for Democracy Pact, took office as president. This pact included the Socialist Party, the Party for Democracy (PPD), the Radical Party and other lesser forces such as the

Christian Left and the Humanist Party. Aylwin exercised a mandate worked out by agreement, based on the willingness of the parties that supported him to put aside their party interests and allow for a supra-party government. At the end of four years of Aylwin's mandate, the Pact was again faced with the task of naming a candidate for the presidency. After consulting the PDC rank and file, the candidature of Eduardo Frei Ruiz-Tagle was put forward, while the Socialist and PPD parties claimed their right to contend for the presidency representing the Pact, and so they proposed the undisputed leader of the left-ist forces in the Pact, Ricardo Lagos. After a procedure was designed to solve this dispute between the two candidates, Eduardo Frei Ruiz-Tagle came out ahead and the Pact won the election with its Christian Democrat candidate, who won over 58 percent of the votes, and this time the mandate was for six years.

Although Frei has completed over half of the period of his presidency, the approach of the next presidential election (1999) is already making itself felt in most of the political decisions made by the Pact parties (and their right-wing opponents): support of, or adjustments to, laws, profiles of potential candidates, and open discussion on how to choose the next representative of the Pact. Although everyone agrees that the important thing is to guarantee President Frei a successful government, there are also those who voice the opinion that it is not too early to design the procedure for nominating the candidate. But beyond this, the dispute continues as to the "greater" rights of one party over another to produce someone from their ranks to represent the Pact in the presidency. The PDC insists that its claim is stronger, since it is the majority party, while Socialists and members of the PPD insist on the need to alternate such a high post. They maintain that it cannot be the numerical majority that imposes such representation, inasmuch as they all constitute a party coalition with a common program. Meanwhile, it is interesting and curious that one of the secondary pacts within the Pact (a modality adopted to maximize the electoral results because of the electoral system in effect) is comprised of the Christian Democrat Party and the Radical Social Democrat Party, the two parties under study here.

According to Scully (1995: 136), the new role played by the Christian Democrat Party as a shaper of coalitions and the arrangement of pacts between the center and the left (thereby reversing a mutual historic antagonism) allows us to speak of a change in the pattern of competition, from a polarized to a moderate type of pluralism.

The PDC Formal Structure

The PDC has both territorial and a functional structure. The territorial one is as follows:

- It begins with grassroots or district activists selected by the district council.
- The provincial councils with their provincial president, elected by province activists.
- The party governing board composed of: the party president, five vice-presidents, a general secretary, a treasurer.
- The Party National Council elected by the junta; the council members may or may not be members of the Assembly; names are proposed and the council members are elected.
- The National Assembly [*Junta*]: the assembly is composed of the Party Council, the Party Governing Board, the provincial presidents, members of parliament and the delegates elected to the Assembly. These are elected by province. The Assembly has a total of 400 people. Assembly meetings are closed, not open to the activists or the public. The Assembly determines and presents the guidelines for the whole party. According to an informant, such meetings are like a liturgy, with two days of listening to speeches by the participants.
- The Supreme Tribunal, which is responsible for resolving conflicts with party discipline.

The functional structure consists of Departments and Fronts. Examples of departments are those for Women and for Shantytown Dwellers. The two fronts are for youth and workers, who are organized into branches.

The first two levels (district and province) are selected by the party activists. The Assembly, Council, and Boards are chosen by systems with several combinations: direct election, appointment, appointment alone, and so forth.

In the opinion of informants, the party is galvanized for elections that are not internal to the party but in competition with other parties, all its cadres teams go into action, they put on party T-shirts and work feverishly to win votes for their candidates. This activity is however not free of conflicts, starting with the nomination of the candidates. In internal elections these are generally local (district, province) leaders, or in the case of the general council, national leaders, who have their own network of neighbors, friends, adherents of the same tendency, and so forth. According to our informants, the leaders must prove their legitimacy by meeting several standards: personal disinterestedness, coming up from the ranks, loyalty, irreproachable family life, and so forth. In short, they should be exemplary activists who have proven themselves in their work, who therefore inspire trust in their comrades. Other conflicts are generated naturally in the course of the electoral campaigns and in terms of the next election, because inevitably there are winners and losers. The animosities that spring from the heat of an electoral struggle are not always easily overcome, nor is it forgotten who provided support to whom.

Just as conflictive or even more so is the nomination of candidates for non-party based national elections. There are squabbles between local leaders and metropolitan ones, too many claimants for the limited number of so-called "places" and equally important, the positions of different party tendencies resulting in complicated negotiations where the leadership attempts to match the preferences of the rank and file with the party's needs, particularly vis-à-vis its coalition allies. This aspect of the negotiations has become more acute with the appearance of two new factors: first, the new electoral law of a binomial nature which does not allow for the presentation of more than two candidates for the places to be filled; and second, the pro-coalition position of the PDC, which forces it, despite its position as the largest party in the country, to surrender positions in order to adjust a candidate list to satisfy the aspirations of its allies. Here we see a repeat of the longstanding internal struggle within the PDC between those who advocate the party having its "own path" and those who tend to make alliances and negotiate. This dispute is not always resolved positively, and hence the leadership has to impose sanctions on those who sidestep discipline and, based on their following, insist upon being nominated or immediately withdraw from the party rather than ceding the position that they regard as theirs, or those who do not observe guidelines that commit them to support other candidates (in elections for mayor, for example).

The formal structure described above derives from the informal structures that gave rise to the PDC and that are revealed in party activity. The next section is devoted to describing such structures and/or networks.

STRUCTURE IN INFORMAL GROUPS

As we have already seen, the early history of the PDC clearly illustrates the formation of informal networks or groups that still constitute the informal base of the party up to this day. These networks, comprised of generational cohorts that share a social and political ideology and subculture, are formed in the places where people come together, such as high school, university, study circles, or groups gathered around Catholic thought, and family ties. The leaders of these networks emerge in a relatively spontaneous way. As networks grow, with the social, cultural, or ideological social distances that may develop between them, currents, tendencies, sensibilities, and factions form, possibly leading to political machinery controlled by what are called "operators." "They are informal networks which operate through a formal structure," says an informant. That is, they work to place their people in the leadership bodies from which they can influence the party's direction—in short, to obtain power. One informant describes it: "There is in the beginning an effort to bring people together with other people that I have already met—at this point we're all from the farming sector. But I keep all my ties with people from the Institute of Christian Humanism, and at some point they invite us as a group—I mean, to join the PDC. The youth of the Institute of Humanism, people from the group of the Federation of University Students (FEUC), and the group from the Federation of the University of Chile Students (FECH), we all converge, groups with different leanings, into the PDC."

Thus the PDC displays the same general pattern of Chilean political culture, where one can observe a certain predominance of the horizontal relationships over the vertical within the social classes (where sociability based on friendship and/or ideological affinities gives rise to the formation of horizontal social networks that ultimately take shape as political bodies or in joining an already existing one). Within the PDC there are various networks where mutual changes take place between members of the same social class. The problem arises with the multiclass situation, which now typifies the PDC and which distorts the ideal model, how things should be, the relationship of equal exchange between comrades. It is resolved with the emergence of horizontal and egalitarian networks on every social level (working class neighborhoods, peasant groups, students, districts), even though the class differences typical of the social structure and Chilean political subculture persist at the party level.

To return to the network structure, it is common to all Chilean political parties: from the wide network of individuals, narrower and more specialized networks (political networks) are concentrated, and they may become formalized as political parties, within which favors, communication, loyalties, and resources are exchanged. Likewise within the parties as they grow, there develop cohorts or networks of generation-linked friends, whose internal structure is egalitarian and highly emotional, and as a rule such networks are formed among young people.

Within these generation-linked networks emerge "natural" leaders, one of whose characteristics is their continual need and ability to maintain their legitimacy within their peer group. Some of these leaders transcend the primary network, and reach other hierarchical levels within the party, even attaining the highest posts, always having to prove themselves as leaders and earn the acceptance of the rank and file. At the same time, and because the party is not homogeneous and also because of political differences, and for generational reasons, and because they belong to friendship groups, currents and factions are produced which in turn shape their "machines," managed by what in political jargon are called "the operators," who work to place their own people in the different leadership positions and to designate candidates for non-party elections.

When this does not happen, fissures occur, factions develop, and groups break off to form new parties (or at least there are rivalries that upset smooth party functioning and even hurt its electoral possibilities). The result is the factionalism typical of Chilean political culture, which has also occurred in the PDC with the separation of the MAPU group during the Frei administration.

This striking prevalence in Chile of trust-based horizontal relationships implies the possibility that access to power is facilitated by structures more like horizontal than vertical networks. Nevertheless, no complex social system can do without the latter. Leaders are indispensable, and hence there arises in Chile a situation that is difficult to resolve, inasmuch as hierarchy or leadership runs counter to the ideal of horizontal networks and the growth of parties.

The characteristics of the relationship between leaders and followers is directly related to the nature of Chilean political culture, and it makes it necessary to respect the horizontal and vertical networks accepted by consent and formalized in law. Monopoly of power by one party or individual would destroy the social peace based on Chile's characteristic multiparty ne-gotiation and coalition system. In accordance with our hypothe-sis on Chilean political culture, hierarchy (or leadership) is in conflict with the growth of horizontal groups (the parties). The result of this dynamic is "factionalism," as a mechanism that limits the growth of hierarchical structures and prevents person-alistic leadership from taking firm hold, except for the legiti-mate leadership of the president of the country, which is sub-ject to criticism. The resulting factions are generally composed of a small number of people representing a group of friends who belong to leadership levels in the party.

4

Party Subcultures

As we have seen, the starting point for organizing political parties is the formation of informal networks based on trust and common interests which become formalized in party structures generally representing a social class, a life-style, and a characteristic ideology that acts as a glue and allows movement across the class boundaries of the initial grouping. The upshot is a group identity based on a life-style, a formal party organization with its own ideology: in short, a group with its own subculture.

The social spaces that the political collectivities come to occupy—comprising networks of friends, family, schoolmates, generation-linked cohorts, neighborhoods, and so forth, plus the related values, symbols, rituals, tastes, and behavior, all bound by a common ideology—this is what makes them a kind of subculture. Its characteristic features that make it recognizable derive as much from the members as from the unit. Who has not heard the phrase "He behaves like a Radical," or "He is a typical Christian Democrat"? A kind of stereotype of others is thereby created, by the way others see them and vice versa, all of which provides ongoing feedback, thus preserving their own separate identity and lifestyle. For their part, those who belong to this subculture feel a strong affinity with their ideological and cultural peers and they have a strong sense of belonging.

A way of life is developed which includes external symbols such as clothes, the schools to which children are sent, women's personal appearance, language, even taste in food. It is all these life-styles that create invisible boundaries which mean that over time there are families or persons of "such-and-such a culture," even if they no longer belong to the political parties in question.

Something more should be said about the class ingredient in the formation of cultural characteristics in political groupings. In the cases under study, the Radicals more clearly share a way of life, by belonging to the same social class, while the PDC multi-class situation means that the Christian Democrats are united not so much by a common life-style as by their humanist Christian ideology, and especially their Catholicism. That is why that ideology is more central to their shared values than concrete life experiences.

The subcultures are related to aspects of being Chilean, with social class, and with the life-styles and ideologies that the groups have developed.

RADICAL SUBCULTURE

"Being Radical is a way of life"

Studying Chilean party politics through the notion that they constitute real subcultures entails determining the social and economic space that they occupy or have occupied, the life-styles that they have developed, the values dear to them, their public and private discourse, the symbolism and rituals that express and reinforce them, and, by way of corollary to all these things, the perception that others have of them, or they have of themselves.

As it sees itself, the Radical Party represents the character of the national culture with its specific characteristics of egalitarianism and horizontality. Its cult of friendship, its willingness to compromise, its inclination to cultivate play and sports, all mesh with the characteristics of middle-class Chileans. Many Radicals believe that "to be Radical is to be Chilean." Another informant declared: "by contrast, we were an essentially national party, with absolutely Chilean features." Speaking of the successful rise and spread of the Radical Party, another one explained: "I have the impression that the party represented a sensitivity that was widespread in the country, because deep down it resonated somewhat with what is characteristic of Chileans."

Interviews with Radicals likewise reveal how strongly activists associate the history of the party with the development of Chile. The achievements of radicalism, particularly those related to education, separation of the church and state, and the economic development of the country, occupy an important place in the way Radicals, then and now, view their party.

An informant who was a major party leader offered the following vision: "A Radical has an open spirit, is democratic, progressive, nonsectarian, has a tendency towards universality, has a particular philosophy of life learned in the Masonic lodges; brotherhood and tolerance are the most fundamental aspects of Masonic life." Pursuing this idea, the same informant observed that Chile has a culture of tolerance that may well have come from the Radical tradition.

Particularly appreciated is the role played by radicalism in the development of education in Chile. Radicals believe that teachers—at one time most of them were Radicals—felt themselves to be "real educators, not only of people but also of the country's civic conscience, which made possible the continued existence of this republican system which we shall never cease praising." "Radicalism initially was concerned—and perhaps this is somewhat characteristic—with cultural matters and teaching," stated a well-known Radical.

The development and expansion of state-funded education is seen as what made possible social mobility and the rise of the middle class, which could thereby acquire or increase its cultural capital. Those Radicals interviewed, most of them children of Radicals and many of Radical teachers, are unanimous in defending the "Teaching State," [*"Estado Docente"*] to which they owe the chance to receive an education. One of them, whose mother was a teacher and father a bureaucrat who started on the lowest rung of the Treasury ladder, compares that situation with the one now: "if we were to examine the possibilities of a government official, who starts out like that today, and is married to a teacher, they would have no chance that their children would attend the university." Another one, speaking of his father, a Radical railway worker, said that his father studied at the Railway Institute. "He could have this kind of education even though he came from the modest middle class."

Appreciation for state-sponsored high schools is a constant. They were created long before the Radicals headed a government, but they are associated with the emergence of the middle class and its needs. In the opinion of one interviewee, the roots of the secular orientation of the "Teaching State" come from some time ago and are tied to the social aspects of the government of Balmaceda, and to the foundation of the Pedagogic Institute of the University of Chile in 1891. However, he emphasizes that it was the Radical thinkers that insisted on hiring several German academics, who put their imprint on the work of the Pedagogical Institute of the University of Chile, which trained many educators well known throughout Latin America. "These founders came and established the structure of the state high school, they imported all the teaching tools from Germany, all these visual aids, they established small museums, physics laboratories, chemistry laboratories, and so forth," recalls one of the informants.

"If I mention my father " says another, "it is only to make it clear that he was a product of the Teaching State. He was naturally of a secular mindset, a Mason, and as such a deist . . . who believed as an article of faith that service to education was an obligation of the State."

Leadership

Traditionally Radical leaders have been, or aspired to be, tribunes, inasmuch as the path to securing a leadership position was by achieving prominence standing out in their speeches to party assemblies at their grassroots organization. Of course, this did not mean that they did not have to show the qualities of any leader: intellectual capacity, coherence in their ideas and actions, charisma, power of conviction, and so forth.

Speaking about the late Radical leader, Luis Bossay, an informant referred to his "weight," explaining why the Chilean Social Democracy to which he belonged, a splinter from the PR during the government of the Popular Unity, could not unite the Radicals led by Enrique Silva Cimma. Among the reasons was "Bossay's weight—Bossay was too big in Chilean politics, and the Radicals were afraid of surrendering to him." (This is an example of the lack of confidence in a leader who is too strong). When Bossay died, however, Social Democrats and Radicals *did* join forces since Bossay's motives to oppose the union were "personalistic." "In a speech . . . it is very easy to be an enemy of joining forces by recalling old offenses, particularly when it is not necessary because the elections are far off." On the other hand, the Social Democracy to which the informant belonged "rejected any idea of reaching an understanding with the group of the Radical Party that had become Marxist-oriented, i.e., Anselmo Sule's group." In fact, his opinion is that the unification did not work out "for personal reasons." Speaking specifically about leaders, this informant believes that lacking "political experience because one has started at the top rather than the bottom" should disqualify such a person from political leadership, although he admits, with regard to Bossay, that "his public speaking was irresistible, and that he could deal with any problem quite competently . . . he was a learned man, a politician out in front, and modern."

Another old Radical activist says that "one of the factors which I believe has a lot of influence on Chilean leaders (and

there are few leaders) is *envy.* Chileans are envious by nature."
To illustrate this statement he describes a cartoon of a competition between three men from different countries who have
to climb a greased pole: a German, an Englishman, and a
Chilean. We see how the Germans and English enthusiastically
cheer on their compatriots while five of his fellow citizens
were hanging on to the Chilean's jacket and pulling him down.
"I said, this drawing is like Chilean society, because here we
don't push up (but we pull down on their jacket)." Although he
recognizes some leaders in Chilean history, they were not leaders in "the way that we understand as a type, let's say, like
Mussolini, like Hitler himself, people like that . . . because
that's what I would call a leader: It is someone who brought out
an idea and they fought for it and they were victorious for it,
and it cost them their lives," Nor does he recognize as leaders
two important Radicals who reached the presidency of the
Republic: Juan Antonio Rios and Gabriel Gonzalez Videla. Of
the first Radical president, however, he says, "I am of the opinion that Don Pedro Aguirre Cerda became a leader because he
had always had this thing of becoming president inside him . . .
but to achieve it—and this is what I consider to be exemplary
about Don Pedro—he devoted himself to studying the country's
problems."

A young informant describes the path to upper-level leadership: being a secondary school, university, trade, or district
leader. "This is more or less your route as a leader, and then
you begin to receive all this political formation from being involved in activities, being in charge of groups of people, plus
the intellectual preparation that you get. This gives you the
chance to move on to the second step, which is to participate at
a party level, at the "upper circles of the party."

In the most recent PR internal elections, in early 1995,
Jaime Campos, a former Radical member of congress, ran for
president against Anselmo Sule, who was seeking reelection.
Campos declared that he had entered the electoral battle because his fellow party members had come to believe that the

party "was passing through an obvious stage of political decline and marginality, due to today's leaders." His chief criticism has to do with the party's weakened role in the Pact for Democracy, the governing coalition. According to Campos and the candidates on his list, the party's present situation is "the result of blind direction and lack of guidelines, that has made it normal for the party to have no proposals and no profile." Among the ideas they advocated was that of approaching the regions and encouraging secular thinking in the cultural domain.

The third candidate to the PR presidency in this election, Sergio Wartemberg, openly supported abandoning the Pact and facing the 1996 municipal elections alone. His criticism of the party leadership, headed by Sule, was that "because of extreme loyalty to the official coalition, his group had been unable to serve as a 'constructive critic' of the government and differentiate itself from the rest of his coalition partners." According to the press, Wartemberg blamed this lack of a clear position not only on the Pact, but also on the national party leaders who preferred to satisfy their "personal aspirations" instead of serving the group.

The candidate for reelection, Anselmo Sule, attacked Campos for declaring that the PRSD was "the last wagon in the Pact." Sule insisted that his party's "only agreement" was with the Pact, and hence the previous electoral coalitions with the PDC "were only administrative and not political." Abandoning the bellicose tone used by his opponents when questioning his leadership, Sule stated, "I should like to repeat that we don't want a confrontation with any of the candidates on other lists. On the contrary, we have a lot of affection and respect for them. We will discuss any differences with them within the party and we invite them to a family party, and family parties take place at home, not in a public square."

In the elections Anselmo Sule's list won with 57.2 percent, with 30.5 percent going to Campos and 8.8 percent to Wartemberg.

Realms of Sociability:
School, Freemasonry, and the Radical Club

School

Because of the Radical commitment to education, early recognition of its importance, and the achievement of a universal, secular public education system, the school and the university became the natural environment for developing social networks and recruiting Radicals. Most of the informants recognized the schools and the activities of teachers as the great school for free thinking, tolerance, broad viewpoints, respect for other people's thinking, and for learning "civic behavior" which is reflected in a willingness to serve the country disinterestedly. Another informant said that his father became a Radical through the influence of his high school and university, and the culture learned from books and theory. He speaks of how his father, an outstanding teacher and supporter of the Teaching State, greatly influenced his life, and, although he is not a Radical, he says with feeling, "We were raised in this environment of people who believed in lay education, who strove to make their school the best, who were proud to be part of an outstanding institution."

In his eulogy to public education, Don Alejandro Rios Valdivia remembers that "the school was the focus of attraction for the middle class (at all levels) and the action precisely of the Radical spirit. Its great triumph was to introduce lay education, the result of which was that the school formed us in a middle-class spirit with a sense of freedom, not tied to dogma, particularly religious dogma" (verbal communication).

Freemasonry

It is easy to recognize the overlap with Masonic principles, which the Radicals by no means deny but actually claim. There was mutual feedback between Masonic meetings and Radical assemblies and they were the true schools of thinking for new recruits. Outside of its lodges, Freemasonry also offered social environments to the young men in Radical circles.

"Almost all of us belonged to lay youth associations, which were para-Masonic institutions and many of us joined the Masons very young due to the fact that we were drawn to the issue of laicism," says another informant, who helped to "form an extraordinarily large Radical group" in the Barros Arana Boarding School, where he studied.

The Radical Club

The Radical Club was, and perhaps still is (since the network of clubs has reassembled throughout the entire country) the paramount location where historically the Radicals' spirit of togetherness, playfulness, and friendship has found expression. Among the propositions of the Radical Club, proclaimed when an association with the name of Radical Club was established in Santiago (*Revista Radical*, no. 1, April 1932, Santiago) are: "to strive for the enlightenment, entertainment, gathering, and daily communication of its members, and the spread of Radical ideas, which will always be based on respect for the Constitution and legislation, and on improving them when they damage or disturb right and liberty in any of the spheres of human activity." The manner for fulfilling these proposals is then set forth. The Club will

1. Every day make available to its members rooms for reading, discussion, and entertainment;
2. Provide conferences on fixed days and on themes accepted by the Board;
3. Serve them in their material needs, and it will especially serve the aims of union and harmony among the country's Radicals;
4. Aid and cultivate relations with similar associations in the provinces and defend its fellow members, when they so request, in matters related to their institution.

The Radical Club soon went on to be the equivalent of a party headquarters, with the particular features that are apparent in the intentions described above. Thus an announcement for the Radical Club in Santiago, published in the *Revista Radical*, No. 9, January 1933, reads:

RADICAL CLUB
Political home for all Radicals in Chile.
Library, billiard room, restaurant, bar.
Lunch and Dinner.
Orders taken for banquets.
Signed by the Administrator.

These characteristics also made the Radical Club a place for entertainment and good food for those who did not belong to the Radical Party. Especially in the provinces, many informants speak of the Radical Club as a place to meet friends, including non-Radicals. The father of an informant frequently went to the Radical Club: "At that time—the '30s, '40s, '50s—everyone went to the Radical Club, whether they were Radicals or not, because the food was good." Another informant, a Radical of provincial origin, remembers that "There were Liberals, people from any party, who went to the Radical Club because they were friends of my crowd." For most informants the Radical Club served a social purpose. One said, "We didn't have splendid homes; all our party activists were middle-income people, very few came from the upper classes; as such they needed [places] . . . to get together because they couldn't get together in their own living rooms, since they couldn't provide food or offer drinks; that wasn't the case on the right." Moreover, he recalls, "For us, political life takes place within social life, in gathering places, which, besides being a regional forum, offered a chance for human exchange, having a good party, a good conversation over a bottle of wine and excellent food." Another informant, the son of a Radical although not one himself, says "the Radical Club expresses a set of customs different from those of the Christian Democrats, who had no equivalent PDC Club."

Thus, in Radical ideology, values are strongly tied to forms of sociability and its concomitants. Commenting on the friendly and hospitable character attributed to Radicals, one of the main leaders stated "That's really the way it is; whenever you arrive, wherever it is, this is what you are going to find. That is why there are also other points that are more of a reflection on the characteristic principles or ideology that identify us. Ours is a rationalist, secular, and humanist party. People say that a Radical is a Radical, a fireman, and Mason—that always gets a laugh. But this is a reflection of those ideas: as a Radical, he is a rationalist; with his sense of solidarity, he lends his services as a fireman; and he is a Mason, because the basic principle of secularism is embodied there in the principle of the search for truth and of the spiritual principles of the defense of the human being, and so forth. But essentially he is tolerant."

A well-known Radical from the time when the party was at its peak, when asked to indicate the main values in his family, emphasized the importance given to the moral quality of others. He added that, more because of his mother than his father, Catholic influence was heavy, and hence it was strange that "a few of us turned out free-thinkers." Another informant underlines the humanist character of the Radical "with a basic foundation from the family for the whole conceptualization of values and principles that aimed at bettering man himself." He insists that the family concept "is very rooted in all that philosophy of thinking and friendship." He believes that there is "a strong reflection of Masonry and its principles." Central to Radical ethical ideas, according to another informant, are "the ways that families live together, all that is connected with friendship, helping one another, as a way of life, almost as an ideology." He states that the sense of brotherhood is learned in Masonry. One informant points out that for a member of a Radical family like his it is unusual not to have continued with university studies. One of his uncles did not go to the university, "in contrast with all his brothers, [who did go] for whom education was not a way to rise socially but rather a way of living a better life. A way of better serving society." In his "Radical family, going to mass was 'useless.'" It did not have the value which his Catholic mother and grandmother attributed to it. An older informant recalls the influence of his grandfather in the formation of values in his generation, entirely through conversations overheard; the importance of study and respect for others even though "they only wear sandals." This democratic character of the party, according to another opinion, is the raison d'etre of Radical respect for the law. "It goes along with feeling democratic, he says; democracy has to be founded on law, and the PR was attached to the law because it was democratic."

Only one interviewee referred explicitly to the aspiration for social justice. He states that his father was a typical representative of what was Chilean middle-class thinking, and that he also represented the nation's teaching profession, the man who searched for a state of liberty, a plainly democratic expression, but along with this "keeping in mind the need for a state not only of well-being, but that there be a state of social justice in the economic realm, that wealth be distributed as widely as possible."

On the other hand, to be a freethinker, and a defender of secularism, has been one of the strongest cultural characteristics of Radicalism. That was what gave rise to the battle for civil marriage, lay cemeteries, public education not subject to the mandates of the church, and so forth. The idea today is quite blurry. One relatively young informant thought that this was partly because the church has adopted the term (laicism) and has its own lay collaborators. Another is of the opinion that there are many secularly-oriented people active in the PDC: "They are somewhat on loan there." Others that should have been Radicals, he says, are in the Socialist Party (PS) or in the Party for Democracy (PPD) "but none of these parties has had the traditions, this sense, this sensibility that the PR represents." He believes that the party should be revitalized, perhaps federated, and new forces should be brought in to "revitalize a kind of thinking that I think the country needs today." For him, "the biggest contribution that Radicals have made and could still make is this contribution of secularism made by Radicalism."

Today (in the '80s and because of the stance of the Chilean Catholic Church toward the dictatorship) most informants do not regard secularism as a special banner for the Radical cause: "the church naturally began to change those old ideas and today they have a greater tolerance than before." But a Radical woman teacher thinks that the PS and PPD should take up the defense of secularism.

A word frequently mentioned by the interviewees represents one of the virtues most appreciated by the Radicals: tolerance, which is linked to brotherhood. That it is not just a word for them is exemplified in a variety of ways. Naturally, there are many Radicals married to Catholic women. An important leader, during the interview, put forth this challenge: "Examine the history of Radicals who have had important posts and I assure you that you are going to find 80 percent married to Catholic women." In his opinion, the struggle against the clergy, essential in the Radicalism of the last century "took place because the clergy maintained a very anti-rationalist, anti-secularist, and anti-Masonic posture, but the tolerance that characterized Radicals did not characterize the clergy of that period." Another informant, a teacher married to a Christian Democrat, points out that there has never been a problem on this count since "we have concentrated on the things that can bring us closer, not the things that can divide us." He adds that, in his opinion, it is helpful that both are from the same social background and that they are both products of public basic education: she from a teacher training school and he from the government secondary school. Another informant who related that he was married to a Christian Democrat "to the daughter of a PDC family, which is also typical of the Radicals; since one of the most outstanding things about the Radicals is, I would say, their lack of sectarianism." He states that he does not understand how one can go through life with a specific pair of glasses "that keeps us from seeing the whole panorama," and he ends by advocating "a great spiritual liberty." His children are being educated in Catholic schools, and that "is another characteristic of the Radicals and the Masons, that we are tolerant." However, and perhaps for this very reason, he believes that his children are going to have "a Radical spirit," and be "broadminded." Another interviewee remembers that her "Radical family" did not keep her from religion and that her father did not stop her from making her first communion, "and when I had a mystical attack he did not stop me either." She is grateful for having been brought up with "complete intellectual freedom (an open library, no prohibitions and, even as a woman, with the emphasis on intellectual worth over the physical)."

Intimately tied to this concept of tolerance is that of "broad-mindedness," which most of our informants see as characteristic of the Radical Party. "Not looking at the color" of people when forming a friendship with them, is translated to the human and political field. An exiled Radical stresses that "the PR is not sectarian; it helps all Chileans regardless of their political affiliation." In his opinion, this sense of brotherhood comes from "ideological training, the Masonic lodge transfers it to the party, which takes it on as its own life-style, which is linked with political practice." Connected to it is the aspect of mutual help; friendships are formed, "people begin to help one another." Here it should be noted that just as it is false to suppose that the PR foundered because it came into existence to fight the clergy and this was accomplished, it is equally false that the PR is a "mutual aid society." That notion, he believes, distorts the situation. "Many would say that when an exile is in difficulties he turns to a Radical, because he knows that the latter will help without asking which party he belongs to." And later on he adds, "that is, breadth is a kind of characteristic of the party. When someone turns to the party, he is never asked where his allegiance lies. It has happened the same way in exile." A "very transcendental vision in life" is the way another informant describes the capacity to recognize that someone else can also be right. For him, relativism allows him not to be absolute in social and political relationships, to accept that "I don't own truth. I recognize that truth can also be divided into portions, among different people, and accepting this leads one to the possibility that others can be right at any given

moment." Another informant sees the "condition of an ongoing full play of ideas, with absolute respect for all beliefs
and fundamentally for sectors that may be in a minority" as
being part of essential Radical Party principles from its very
beginnings.

Also deeply rooted in Radical culture is another characteristic, closely related to the ideas of tolerance and broadmindedness. This is respect for other people's ideas, and even more, a
consistent stance of not influencing other people's decisions,
considering the freedom of individual decision to be a privilege
that inherently belongs to every person. This trait appears as a
constant in the informants' statements, both as a principled
stance of Radical humanism, and in the relations of Radicals to
their friends and family. Most informants admitted having
been influenced by the family environment in their becoming
Radicals but they always stressed that their fathers had never
pressured them or even suggested that they join the party. "It
was fundamentally through example, we were never pushed,"
declared one of them. An example of the importance given to
respect is offered by an informant when he remembers that his
father, a history teacher, directed him towards the Radical
Party in a "very subtle and gentlemanly fashion." Indeed, he recalls that when, while still in secondary school, he told his father that he wanted to join the party, his father replied, "I'm
afraid that you may be influenced by me, so I don't think it
would be a good idea for you to decide at this particular time.
See first of all what the other parties are like, try to get information from other people, from your friends." According to the
informant, what his father said greatly affected his life, since
"he showed me one of the greatest values, one that I most admire in Radicalism, namely, respect for everyone, and why
each one reaches his truth through his or her own reflection."
Another states categorically that "the Radical is essentially tolerant. And being tolerant he does not mind whether his son is
Catholic or not, it does not worry him. He leaves it up to the
son to make up his own mind, and he doesn't pressure him."

Life-Style

A good deal of the Radical way of life comes from its provincial origins. "The PR, as I have observed it, is very much a regional party, it is a party that is based on family relations and friends from childhood. There was a stage in Chile when people were educated and spent their adolescent years in the provinces," says an informant. This feature is mentioned repeatedly by most of those interviewed. It also marked the Radical Party from the outset, almost as a counterpart to the principles mentioned above. Life is centered on the family, but in the provinces one knows everyone; one's friends are colleagues, neighbors, parents of the children's school friends, the major figures in the town or city, regardless of their political tendencies. When speaking about the Radical Club, the institution that became well known in the provinces, everyone describes it as a place for meeting friends "of any political hue" (to play, drink, and talk). All the major occasions are shared not only with family but also with friends. An informant illustrates this by relating that when in one house a *pastel de choclo* [a kind of corn pie] was made or some other festive or appetizing meal was made in anyone's house, friends were always called in to share it. Another emphasizes that the provincial social relationships (among Radicals) occurred strictly within the middle class. He says that the provincial oligarchy is much more narrow-minded than in the capital, precisely because it is more nouveau riche, and not so pure. Another, from a Radical family, speaking of the enduring relationship that migrants to the capital maintained with their birthplace, uses an illustrative metaphor: "And this type of relationship reproduces an internal relationship native to the provinces, where the petite bourgeoisie of the town or a larger city is a family, a tribe, a clan, where people keep in touch through family ties, local origin, through contact based on studies."

The way the interviewees describe their social life fits with that of the historian Gonzalo Vial when he describes the entertainment of the early Chilean middle classes: country walks, strolls around the city squares (in their neighborhoods) dances, social gatherings, games, parties in houses where the host "spared no expense"; they danced waltz, polka, and square dances. They dined lavishly" (Vial, 1981, vol. 1: 700).

Another interviewee remembers that his father had "lots of friends; many of them basically friends from work; they weren't political friends." Family social life was expressed basically around sports, but that was only one part, "The other, the social part, the typical affair of the barbecues . . . we're talking about the countryside. Besides that, lots of social activity, birthday parties, what have you."

A Radical interviewed in exile declared that, in his opinion, "what was lost (after the military coup) was the space for daily life, the daily lifestyle that was reproduced even in the city, the provincial ways of life . . . a style of personal relations between people which included, of course, a quite distant relationship, perhaps an ironic one, with politics. Above all, there was this provincial tranquility in our daily life, where we maintained clan and family values." He remembers his father's friendships in a northern city, the doctors, important people, wealthy tradesmen, "but there was no sharp ideological separation for him as a Radical, as far as his friendships were concerned. He entered these circles as a member of the middle class, not as a Radical, that is, he didn't distinguish between those who were priests, or those who were Catholics, and those who were not. . . ." He adds, "They continued to be friends and joke around, but around the barbecue and at a family situation, getting together, going out, forming a group for the spring festival."

Social activity is always associated with specific dishes or with good food in general. Even though some Radicals reject the idea of being associated with "the art of fine food" and eating particular delicacies of Chilean cooking, most are quite willing to agree that Radicals are fond of making political and social contacts over a good meal. When a new Radical Club opened in Santiago, an important party figure was good-naturedly shocked to discover that the club was vegetarian, "which has nothing to do with the Radical mindset." In his opinion, this mindset "is closely related to pickled rabbit, leg of pork, a piece of meat and *causeo de patitatas*, (pigs' feet) and all those delicacies that you would find in any Chilean Radical Club." This is all in addition to the celebration of family festivals or rituals at national fiestas, which in every house, of any political hue, meant a special menu: Sunday *empanadas* (meat-filled pastry), Christmas turkey, the barbecues for the "18th."[1]

In the countryside, an informant remembers the barbecued lamb, poultry raised in one's own yard, and so forth, "Everything very Chilean, where a large part of the attitude to daily life was expressed through food, lots of food, tasty delicacies, good wine, special trips to buy certain kinds of things in certain places." Everyday food, according to one informant, was typical of a middle-class Chilean family, with stews, vegetables, corn, salads, and so forth.

As for Santiago, according to an informant, from the 1930s onward, Radicals were concentrated in certain areas of the city, such as Nuñoa. This informant lived among Radicals and middle-class people. Let us keep in mind that the formal organization of the party was based on the district assemblies.

Another important aspect of the Radical style of life is their formal and fastidious form of dress. According to an outstanding party leader, a Radical always keeps up his style, such as a suit. "At regular meetings it is rare to find a Radical without a tie. Possibly on Saturdays or at extraordinary meetings you could see Radicals dressed informally. But not during their normal meetings." The same informant also stresses the importance given by the head of the National Institute to dress, care of hands and nails, and presenting oneself "as a respectable person, as a person who would be respected by the students." The same preoccupation appears in the interview with an informant whose mother liked to dress well and also dressed her two daughters well. "My mother was showy, and my father liked to be in fashion. Hence, all of my brothers and sisters learned to be *"chutes,"* a term indicating that people are very

1. September 18 is Independence Day in Chile.

careful about their appearance, paying attention to all the details, like their tie, handkerchief, and so forth. "They inherited this because in this regard my father was demanding, and he was also demanding in his personal habits."

Another feature observable in the Radical lifestyle, according to a well-known leader, was that party members worked while studying. "I daresay that rather than for economic reasons this was part of a way of life." Making a comparison with the Christian Democrat Party, he notes that, for example, a high representative of the PDC is, just like him, a typical product of public secondary school, as are many others of the PDC leadership. "Nevertheless, they never had this habit of working at the same time. I think it is part of the way Radicals are."

Radicals regard the family as very important. "The Radical world . . . is one of solid families (even though divorce is accepted nowadays). They are quite conservative." He added that for this reason Radical families withstood exile well, in contrast with others: "The family core, secular education, Masonry all help to provide stability in marriage. . . . It is a family that does not talk about sin or dogma; belief is not mandatory." No Radical family is dogmatic, even when the mother or grandmother is Catholic.

Hence, politics and family life are mixed together in the lifestyle of Radicals, which is well defined although not sectarian. As another interviewee says: "This is what we used to have in our homes, this humanism, a concern on the part of our parents to imbue such values in their children, a love of politics; and the truth is that these people practiced a true priesthood." Another informant, who, although from a Radical family never became one, also remembers that politics was discussed at home. "On Sundays when we met in my grandmother's house, there were extraordinarily good political discussions . . . but they were all Radical except for one uncle." She, who was Catholic as a child, (through her mother) and even made her first communion, "broke" with the Catholic Church in her early teens. She thinks that the only thing that gave her the strength to do this was "reason" and that "this

idea of reason was evidently something I had learned at home."
Her conclusion is that "I had the structural strength that helped
me to make this break without much suffering." Another
member of the same family, also remembers the family table,
where along with food, they imbibed Radical values and political teaching. She says that the new generation, her own, con-
served the ideological tendencies that they acquired this way,
although she qualified, "a little bit more evolved in some
cases, but still Radical; no one is on the right or the extreme
left." She mentions the exception of one family member who
left the center, "but later he changed his mind, and went back
to being center-left."

As can be seen in these examples and others cited above, in
what were called Radical families, the father prevailed ideologically, and although many of the women remained practicing
Catholics and their children were baptized, in political terms
what ultimately prevailed was the father's Radical-Masonic
ideology: rationalism, secularism, and tolerance. As another example of the political influence of fathers over their children,
an informant declares, "During the time of the Popular Unity I
joined the PR through my father's influence—he had joined in
1935. . . . And the public high school also made its impact."
Another informant places a lot of importance on conversations
overheard at home, the background provided by his father on
political developments in Europe, nineteenth century liberal
movements, and the social and political development in Latin
America, and he concludes: "Now I think that he [his father]
could not put aside his activism, even though he wanted to act
very modestly and impartially."

As we shall see, the value and significance that friendship
has for the Radicals merits a separate section. Tolerance, broadmindedness, and respect for others' ideas (characteristic traits
of Radical culture, according to informants), are translated also
into the already mentioned ability to have friends of any hue: "I
do not choose my friends for their political hue," states an informant. The basis of his network of friends goes back to primary and secondary school. A *compadre* (the godfather of one's

child) and friend, also a Radical, was his companion in the youth fraternity, Alpha Phi Epsilon, whose members were "the best students in the secular university," he says. Another remembers that in the northern city where he lived, "the closest friends of my father (a Radical) were people who eventually became PDC. Catholic people, Christians." He remembers that he also got together with the children of these families but that "the older folks got together continually." Radical informants frequently mention "Catholic friends," as both schoolmates and neighbors.

Asked how he would define friendship, a leader of the Radical party replies: "Just as Chileans understand it: withstanding any test, doing favors under any circumstances: we call friendship brotherhood," he explains. Speaking of the rise of the Radical-style friendship, he adds: "being Radical was a way of being human, and it unfolded through the policy of friendship, through service to friends. In Chile this culture become a 'friendocracy'." He recalls that before the coup everything was said to be done that way: "You've got to help him because he's a friend, a good person, a decent 'mummy'" [term of contempt for conservatives] (that is, even if he has another political position). In the opinion of this informant, this attitude ran into crisis with the integralist [insistent upon orthodoxy] tendencies in the PDC and the PC-PS. He stresses that friendship is an instrument of Radicalism, and recalls the case of a municipal council member who was elected not because of his speeches but for having done services for his friends. "We leaders today have been friends since childhood; we visit one another, our children are friends, we have been through the same ups and downs. The leadership bunch in '73 went to the concentration camp on Dawson Island together. We were the most united group there and the most helpful to others. The PDC and the Marxist-Leninists, by contrast were intolerant and integralist."

For Radicals, cultivating friendships is something of a categorical imperative, and it used to lend itself to the accusation that the Radical Party practiced *"amiguismo"* [jobs for friends] and that granting favors to friends turned it into a party where

corruption was rife (Lomnitz, 1971). The accusation of corruption is energetically rejected by a major Radical leader, but
he nonetheless defends *"amiguismo"* and *"compadrazgo"*
[similar but with the implication of adoptive family relation-
ships] as positive characteristics. "The PR was a party that for
many years, and I would say even today, continues to see its interests as connected to the national budget. Why is that? Because of this sense of 'getting a handful.' From work, from the
job, of course there was a lot to be had in the public sector. And
that is where this started—it's not false, it's real. It's not repre-
hensible. Because, I'll tell you, as long as things are equal, okay,
you have the right to decide. I don't think it's unjust to decide
in favor of a person who identifies with your point of view."
About *"amiguismo"* in particular, he says "The Radical party
is a party where *'amiguismo'* continues in the sense that you
create a group of persons who are really your friends around a
shared ideological position." He explains, "They like to sit
around a table, just conversing, or discussing an issue. Why?
You know there's a central point on which there's agreement."
The informant extends this cultural characteristic to Masonry,
where there are many Radicals and adds: "You will see that
after the ritual meetings Masons get together to eat and then
play *cacho* or dominoes, and this is where the overlap or agreement in the way of being of Radicals and Masons comes about."
Likewise, an older informant believes that friendship is something "which forms part of reality and myth" around the development and influence of the PR in creating the Chilean bureaucracy. When asked where this might have come from he
concluded that it came from the PR, "because it had the appropriate education, for cultural reasons; appropriate professional
training and moral formation for public office," besides the obvious source in the teaching profession, (which was Radical).
This informant argues, "Let's look at the Mail and Telegraph
Service (C & T); why haven't well-educated privileged kids
been C and T administrators? For the simple reason that they
were aspiring to other things, from being archbishop on down."
That is why, "public administration is a kind of platform that

forms part of Chilean culture and development, and it was filled fundamentally by folks from the PR." He believes it is an absurdity to distort the use of social networks for getting jobs, by calling it the well-known "Radical serving spoon." On the contrary, he says, the PR filled a need that others were not willing to fill because they "had higher aspirations." Drawing a parallel, he indicates, "Supposing you were accepting applications, for example, for school principal; fifty apply, and forty-five of them are Radicals. It was logical. Just like if you were accepting applications for a position as an economist, probably only five Christian Democrats would apply. It was a different kind of training."

With respect to favors, the historian Gonzalo Vial points out that Radicals and Masons had the same spirit as far as mutual aid is concerned, the former served their party "colleague," the latter their "brother." He adds that this tacit system of mutual aid was typical of the Radical Party, which has always been criticized by its adversaries as a form of corruption (Vial: 135).

Closely connected to the theme of friendship is that of the networks that emerged among Radicals: "We began as a group that was practically formed on its own initiative; many of us were sons of Radicals," relates an old activist who was student and youth leader. He recalled that he was responsible for coordinating ties with "the groups of secondary students that had been emerging in different private and public secondary schools throughout the country."

Public high schools were decisive in the formation of the Radical networks of friendship and politics: "The high school in La Serena is a key point," indicates another interviewee. "My grandfather, my father, and I, all went to the high school in La Serena and both my grandfather and my father established most of their contacts and their relationships there." The informant, who is not a Radical but from a Radical family, stresses how important relationships established while studying were for the development of the PR, "since they were recruiting centers for liberal and anticlerical ideas." Another thinks that his father became Radical through the influence of his work: the

State Railways (Ferrocarriles del Estado); "As it was created entirely by Radicals, he must have been influenced by his work companions, by his bosses, and so forth." This same man, a graduate engineer from what was then the State Technical University, became a Radical and then, "as you gradually learn more, you begin to pass on all this conceptualization [Radical doctrine] and all these principles to your schoolmates." The informant, a student leader, describes his political activity within the university as "trade-related, but translated to the university." This activity was one of making demands, aimed at "being able to have some impact on development, and on your own training." Radicalism had a strong presence in his university, because it was the result of Radical activity (Alejandro Rios Valdivia). "It is a university created by the Radical Party, embodying a whole ideology, a notion of education that is very much ours as Radicals." This informant got his first professional work through the party. The vice-president of the company where he applied for work "was a fellow Radical; so, through this 'friendocracy', as we call it, I started work there." While still in the university he began to work in the youth clans, "which marks the beginning of the formation in values and principles to improve people in their particular worlds in order to then seek to improve society."

Work as a union leader among organized teachers gave another informant strong support in his political career as a congressional deputy, although he says that he has always tried to keep the two activities separate. Hence, when he became a candidate for deputy, he left the board of the National Association of Teachers. In addition to belonging to this association for secondary teachers, he joined the Chilean Union of Teachers for primary school teachers: "I didn't do anything noteworthy there, but it helped me stay in contact with my colleagues." It should be noted that this informant has had an outstanding career in education.

Contacts made at public and private primary and secondary schools and universities are where political friendships and the social and political networks are forged. That is plain from the experiences described here, as well as those of the informants' fathers. One informant who is not a Radical relates that her father became a Radical while at the Barros Arana school. Her father was for many years a well-known politician and Radical member of congress for several terms. When the informant suddenly married a young man who had still not finished his studies in economics, her father obtained a job for him in CORFO (Corporation for Development). Another informant, who was not Radical either, thinks that his father became a Radical at the University of Chile. Although his father studied law and education, he thinks that it must have happened in the Pedagogic Institute, which, in his opinion, "must have been a Radical Party breeding ground."

This morality (of mutual aid), states Vial, set its members, who were middle class, apart from the oligarchic groups whose social and economic position was based on family ties. Vial's conclusion is that the liberal professionals of the middle class also needed a "family" that would secure them a position in the world of work, and they found such a family in Masonic lodges: (Vial, 1981, vol. 3: 137–38).

Ways of Engaging in Politics

This review of the typical features of Radical culture, its tolerance, broadmindedness, respect for others, and the like, suggests that these traits could be at the basis of the PR's willingness and ability to negotiate. "In Chile political problems were resolved by eating at the Radical Club . . . because (Radicals) introduced the human factor. 'Let's not be ideological,' they used to say. 'Let's look at things from the angle that we belong to the same social sector and we're friends; otherwise, how are we going to get ahead? Give up your integralism and your dogmas.'" This informant believes that "this capacity for mediation was why Radicals presided over all the committees of the Popular Unity (in 1970–1973), and those of the Pact in 1989 and 1993 . . . and they do this because they are good friends." It is also significant that shortly after becoming president of the

Republic in 1990, President Aylwin chose Raul Rettig, distinguished Radical jurist and former leader of his party, as president of the Truth and Reconciliation Commission, which was composed of representatives of different political sectors.

Some informants who were student, trade union, and parliamentary leaders explicitly mentioned this attitude of "getting along with everyone." For example, a leader of the teachers' union and later member of congress declared that in this capacity "I never set ideological conditions; I got along with everyone." Another notes how in the struggle against the dictatorship, because they were not "in favor of a violent confrontation because it was absurd," they began to "prepare here—in a combination of parties—to form a broad union of parties to defeat the dictatorship, and it had to be defeated by some legal means." The informant explicitly recognizes the help of the church in the task of looking for "this consensus to search for legal solutions."

Another recalls the role played by the PR, first in "forming and leading the left in 1938 and later in forming the left with the Popular Unity." He believes Radicals played a very important role, because at the outset only the Radicals and the Communists were in favor of this coalition, and the Socialists were opposed. He states that in the first of these two cases, the PR led a coalition on the left, and in the second it was an important part of it. "Because of its political formation the PR is a flexible party and finds it easy to reach an understanding even with right-wing sectors." He believes that this capacity of the PR has also a negative side, proper to the middle class (which is surely going to happen to the PDC). In his analysis, reaching power means that capitalism, the bourgeoisie, will seek contacts with government lawyers, because "the state is everything in developing countries. Thus lawyers, whose names used to be Bulnes, Larrain, Vial [typical surnames of the upper class], begin to take their interests and affairs to the offices of lawyers with government connections."

Another major Radical leader stresses the importance of the PR (as the arbitrator) within the kind of democracy under which democracy unfolds in Chile. "It is the party that essentially shapes the political system compromise-based democracy, in which we all agree to sustain a minimum of values which make it possible for the democratic system to function." Although obviously all the sectors have ideals higher than this compromise "we cede a portion of our ideals to the future, in order to maintain a desirable political system for the country now." Although some, and here he does not exclude himself, have sometimes criticized making political transactions as shameful, looking at it properly, he says: "I think that within politics making deals is one way to engage in politics. The point is to be smart enough to reach an agreement with other political sectors in order to secure a decent situation for all citizens." He emphasizes that from the fall of Ibañez (1931) until 1964 or 1965, the system of compromise-based democracy held sway in Chile, "and the PR played an extraordinarily large part in it." He believes the PR has been the pillar of this system with its human formation, its secularism, and all the values it embodies, tolerance, brotherhood, and so forth. This was achieved "through the way PR activists shared their lives." Currently, in the opinion of an informant, "there is a feeling that there should be a meeting of ideas not a separation and deprivation. And whichever the position is helpful for social development, for the good of Chile, and for education in general, well, groups support one another."

View of Others

Radical informants generally avoided describing, qualifying, or detailing the life-styles of the PDC. Their opinion was rather focussed on defining and/or questioning the political aspect of the question and scarcely referred to the subcultural aspects.

Thus, one informant refers to the part played by the PDC, as spokesman for the ideas of the Alliance for Progress and, as a consequence, in the implementation of the agrarian reform, in the process offending the Chilean capitalist bourgeoisie, who were unable to perceive the importance of the American initiative. "Instead of supporting it, instead of giving in a little, accepting a degree of agrarian reform, accepting some change in the tax system, promoting some state ownership . . . they stayed in their castles and blasted all these initiatives." Likewise, all the PDC initiatives, such as agrarian reform and the "Chileanizing" of large mining operations, he describes as incomplete and insufficient. In the treatment given to these two questions, says the informant, "I think that the PDC shows its character very clearly, ambiguous surely, because it attempts to appease both God and the devil, and ultimately pleases no one." Above all he heavily criticizes the policy on copper, but admits that the PDC government marked an advance within the political evolution of Chile and that Frei Montalva was "one of the greatest statesmen in Chilean politics." With some variations, another informant expresses similar ideas: on the PDC government program, he comments that it was typically reformist, progressive, and forward-looking, and opposed by the bourgeoisie, whose servant Frei ultimately became. He believes that as a young party the PDC "is more sectarian" and "it appears that it did not have the tradition nor the capacity to negotiate."

To this informant the Christian Democrats "have a spiritual composition," and "they are more given to firing blanks and are shyer and more hypocritical. . . . They have a narrow point of view and this is due to their Catholic upbringing."

Illustrating what he calls a "different life-style" (that of the Radical Party as opposed to the PDC) a major Radical figure says that Radicals are typically people "who have shaped themselves through their own work" and notes that young Radicals work while in school (justifying at the same time the role played by the party in obtaining work for their fellow Radicals, since it "is done because of this idea of work"). This trait of working in school, he says, "was not true of the PDC," which was not meant to denigrate it, but simply to point out that it is another approach to life. Because the PR is "a regional party, from the provinces," in this informant's opinion, it is in the provinces where the differences between Radicals and PDC are more obvious. He indicates that in spite of the effort on the part of the leaders to work together politically "believe me, in the provinces it's difficult, because Radicals believe that in the PDC they are facing their enemy, and that the PDC is domineering, imposes its own criteria, and so forth. One of the hardest things is to persuade the Radical grassroots to have faith in the PDC as an ally." Insisting on this point, he admits that "From Arica to Magallanes" one can hear it said that, "These pious men are completely mixed up; you can never trust them." He insists that he does not share this opinion, but at the same time says that when the leaders try to convince the grassroots of the need to work together, they reply, "From the top, things look different, because they react differently, but the moment they can stab you, they will." On the other hand, he believes not only are there groups of friends in the PDC, as in Radicalism, but "I would venture that they are even stronger. I think that friendship among the PDC is utterly more coherent and stronger and more passionate in defending and making efforts for one another than even among Radicals."

Another informant, indicating that the PDC became a middle-class party "when it became the dominant party," explains that, in his opinion, parties in Chile grow at one another's expense. In this case, the PDC capitalized on PR losses. "If at some moment the PR declined, somewhere else there is a connecting line that enabled the other to rise." It does not matter at all that the PR has the lay ingredient and the PDC a religious connotation. "Today many people in the PDC or voters who don't belong to the DC but will vote for it are not practicing Catholics, and they have a secular vision of politics and life and are there nevertheless because it is the majority party"—or because this party gives them the chance of have influence more effectively. Comparing the Radicals and Communists, the same informant points out that the difference lies in the fact that it was typical of Communists that (at least previously) they "woke up Communist, lunched Communist, dined Communist, and dreamed of the Communist Party." This informant, whose wife is a Christian Democrat, insists that he has had no problems with her over politics, because, "The PDC, I would say, as a result of developments in the church, has also opened up; they are less dogmatic, they have a broader criteria, I would say that they have become 'Radicalized' in the sense, not of going to extremes, but rather becoming more like the PR in adopting this spirit of sharing and being tolerant."

A long-time Radical involved in education points to a higher level of academic preparation in the PDC. When analyzing the problem of the loss of young people from the PR, he said: "Why? The PDC came into being because of young educated Christian youth, specially prepared by activists. This broadened and produced politicians such as Frei [Montalva] and all those people, that type of party member." In the 1930s the informant remembers having observed how many young people went to extracurricular classes and how they "stayed behind to discuss with the friars who were very intelligent and it was a lot of fun." As a teacher he saw that after official classes ended, "many youths didn't leave, most didn't go home, but rather went to classes at DESAL." When he asked the director about this, he was told, "we understand that the official curriculum has to be satisfied, but there is not much in the way of philosophy, so we give [special] training to our students who are going to go to the university."

For another informant, the contrast between Radicalism and the PDC is based on the fact that it has "clientele of the same class, from the same sector, but based on a church connection." For him, Radicalism was more important initially, because it answered "the needs and the regional type of contacts," and everything entailed "in terms of loyalties, a system of favors already rendered or expected for other former favors." An informant who joined Radicalism at a time that he describes as "very politicized" (the 1960s) compares his party with the Communist Party. The basic difference between the PR and the PC, he believes, lies in the Communist attitude of a total and abrupt change, which clashes with "some of our more democratic non-confrontational positions." Another informant interprets the rise of the PDC at the expense of the PR as a consequence of the PR "moving rather for immediate interests, not even for long-term interest with broad goals, and that explains the disaster," and that led to the rise of the PDC, which he described as being "typically middle class." He believes that the rise of the PDC, particularly under the banner of agrarian reform, "prompted the candidacy of Jorge Alessandri against that of the PDC Radomiro Tomic" in 1970. In his reasoning, when the PDC was in the opposition "as happens with all the PDCs in the world, they became radicalized. After the failure of the "populist government of Carlos Ibañez, the right wing comes into power, and then, as a third step, the PDC wins with their support, with a program that is not carried out, because bourgeois opposition, and Frei ends up almost as a servant of the bourgeoisie. It is a reformist program, but popular demands go far beyond it." According to him, the PDC used the same means of pressure with the peasants that the right had traditionally used; "they even used a different system which was paternalism." This last term refers to the urban *lumpenproletariat* without "consciousness-raising." He mentions mothers' centers, provision of basic household goods, and so forth. The party attracted the peasants by promising agrarian reform. "They also had the human resources, since it is a class-conscious party, in other words it has powerful landowners and it also had Catholic sectors to help it." This informant was of the opinion that a Christian Democrat can always be detected "within three minutes, because of his sectarianism." At the time of the interview (1980s) the informant saw the PDC as having more radicalized sectors "due to the eleven years of dictatorship, but they are still distinct." By contrast, a Radical is always identified by his expansiveness: "He is a good friend, like a brother, he has an open spirit. One always finds a Christian Democrat to be sectarian, no matter how far along he is." The PDC, in this informant's opinion, has "a tendency, a facility to reach an understanding with the right, as it has done, and not the left, [a temptation that transcends] their ideological reasoning." By contrast, if one takes "any Radical, why is it easier for him to reach an understanding with Communists? Because he belongs to the same circles, has the same customs, does the same things. There may be a political abyss between them but they like red wine by the liter, the same conversation, they enjoy sports, they share a different view of sex, friendship, sin, things that are very important." Comparing the Christian Democrats to Radicals, he emphasizes that the PDC "had no club (like the Radical Club). Of course it had no club, because it had the Church— that's the PDC club. Their church is their center, life runs from Sunday to Sunday, and they are sectarian." He adds that they are so sectarian that the even President Frei [Montalva], recognized that it was a mistake to have governed alone, taking advantage of the parliamentary majority that the PDC obtained. He described the fact of having obtained it as "bad luck," because it meant that he did not have to govern by coalition.

Remembering the varied attempts at forming an alliance in opposition to the dictatorship, another informant speaks of the Communists, whom they could not accept for fear that they would provoke a repeat of the Popular Unity. "Toward the Communist Party our position was always, 'Look, you have to dive underwater, you have to exit from the scene and return later.' But they ignored us, they continued the struggle for a broad front until 1980." When the constitution of 1980 was in place, the PC turned to armed struggle.

In the opinion of a woman informant, a great difference between her and a very close Christian Democrat friend of hers was the her friend's obsession with virginity. "For her virginity was a struggle, and I mean a terrible one. We were already twenty years old. I tried to understand her, because what I told her seemed outrageous, because of the way I didn't prize some things, and how much she prized them, and her piety." Both continue to be great friends but the informant is amazed that her friend is now very concerned over the fact that a nephew is getting divorced. More categorical in her opinion is another older woman informant. Referring to how the rank and file Radical regards the DC, she states "Oh no, horrible. [Christian Democrats] believe that the world revolves around them alone."

Our last informant recognizes that he could not establish ties with a people who are very Catholic. Like Radicals in general, his own life is far from what happens at weekly mass and church social life. When he talks about Radical Clubs as a meeting center for Radicals, he says, "Radical Clubs do not bring religious groups together. Radicals have the same custom of meeting in one another's homes . . . among friends."

We end this section on Radical subculture by citing a significant party leader, who states, "Radical culture isn't going to disappear, because it is the culture of the middle class."

CHRISTIAN DEMOCRATIC SUBCULTURE

"Being Christian Democrat is a way of life"

The common ideological characteristic of the Christian Democrats is Catholicism. Coming from Catholic families, or with a Catholic mother, young high school and university students begin to forge small groups united by faith, and later by their adherence to the church's social doctrine: "My mother was a very religious person and every Sunday we went to mass as a family," says an informant. Another adds: "I entered the party in 1946 primarily because I then belonged to Chilean Catholic Action. During the time of Father Hurtado and Bishop Manuel Larrain, this movement introduced many social concerns to us in Chile; it was a nice school for many Falangists. It gave us strong motivation to belong to a party." The arrival of Vekemans led to the creation of the Institute of Christian Humanism, a group of professionals, generally Catholics in different disciplines and guided by the church's social inspiration, in order to do social research.

Thus, the Christian Democrats constitute a party whose ideals are directly related to Catholic values—hence the Christian conception of the human being, with a strong impulse toward social justice, the PDC regarding itself as an alternative to liberalism and Marxism. In addition, Christian Democrats reject violence on principle. The concept of the community structure of society, or the primacy of the social over the state and the individual, has been a substantial aspect of Christian Democrat ideology, which is expressed, for example, when an activist says: "I joined [the party] for its profound doctrine. It was like seeing myself reflected in what I felt should be a human being with that solidarity that I see, that mystique. I see myself reflected in this party doctrine." In another case, an early perception of a culture of its own coming into being is neatly visible: "What one begins to see is that there are customs, life-styles, values, history." The statement of another interviewee confirms this supremacy of "values" over other positive achievements: "I studied at St. George's school, and graduated in 1962. I belong to the old 'Georgians.' It wasn't that we received such a good education there, but it was a formation in terms of values and leadership, and knowing that one had to excel, and also in social questions, in helping people in poor neighborhoods. We used to read and examine magazines from the standpoint of the Christian message."

Most of the informants note the qualities demanded by being a Christian Democrat, highlighting them with a strong sense of "ought-to-be." One of these qualities is austerity, a quality that an old activist is proud to be able to point to in Christian Democrat leaders: "The early leaders of the DC were very austere. You saw the same austerity when [President] Aylwin hosted George Bush, as when [President] Frei (Montalva) welcomed the Queen of England at his home. I remember the changes in the Frei house when he was going to be president. They added a dining room because there wasn't any." A young informant highlights other aspects of the Christian Democrat "ought-to-be" more directly related to Christian Doctrine, "Perhaps I see the Christian Democrat dividing his time in two. One part is the personal side, which is tremendously important if he wants to handle everything else well, taking care of his life, his work, etc. But the other part of his time is with people. I see him as a happy person, a person with a mystique, who can transmit—

I don't know, some would call it energy, others sentiments, feelings—and I believe that basically it is from a faith viewpoint. This is what any Christian has to do, transmit that; the difference is that we transmit it from a political perspective and we make it perhaps more rational. I see a Christian Democrat as not very materialistic in terms of attachment to material things." An old activist agrees: "I think that the best family is the Christian Democrat family. It is very united, people respect one another a great deal. You can see a lot of love, affection, a lot of concern for one another. Besides, I greatly admire large families and the Christian Democrats are typically very good fathers, very good mothers, and put a lot of devotion into it."

Furthermore, references to the common good and the will to serve are common in Christian Democratic ideology: "This idea that politics is linked to service is a DC idea" not shared by Socialists, states a noted activist. "The idea is ultimately connected to a Christian notion."

"My father viewed service as the main point of his life. He served in politics, he was always serving, everywhere," declares the daughter of a noted Social-Christian. A former Christian Democrat activist says: "My vocation is public service; within the private sector . . . but public service, serving society. I am motivated to do this, it's no merit of mine. It's within me; the search for justice is within me." For an upper class interviewee (from 'the old aristocracy') this willingness to do public service is what marks the cultural difference from conservative families in the same social stratum: "The conservative world is wealthier than the other one, (ours), where the primacy is put on professional public service." It is the world of finance and business, as opposed to that of public service.

The strong sensation of belonging which gives rise to this communion of ideals and the feeling of "we-ness" is clearly expressed in the statement of a former district leader. "As a Christian Democrat, you come to any party location fully confident; no matter where it is, arriving at the party means arriving home."

Leadership

The attributes demanded of Christian Democrat leaders say a great deal about the ideology and the values that the party seeks to represent. The opinions that we have gathered in this work also suggest that changes have occurred in this area and they are not very welcome to the activists we have interviewed, as will be evident here.

In the section on the formal and informal structure of the Christian Democrat Party we spoke of how leaders emerge, a process which normally starts with "natural leaders" who stand out in the various party networks. All informants agreed on their description of Christian Democrat leaders, insisting that they must observe a high standard in moral character, spotless conduct in family and social affairs, and commitment and unselfishness in serving the common good. One of them comments, "My experience is that leaders are born not made. Intelligence is important in a leader; he is well prepared, he radiates something spiritual. But he has to be proper in his behavior, project an image of austerity around himself, have a moral behavior that is an example to the rest, and he must be a good at organizing."

A former leader observed: "Leaders are figures with a large vision, who somehow inspire public trust, the image of being a good father. They are intelligent, likeable, and have a lot of drawing power."

A woman offers her vision: "A leader is a very tenacious person, is always doing something and offering something, and has to be quite intelligent, and to have very clear, very precise ideas."

In the view of a Christian Democrat of the younger generation, there appears a new accent, one that prizes the intellectual capacity of the leaders, and places less emphasis on the moral attributes that older activists find so important: "To me a leader is someone who has his own opinion, who is not anyone's puppet, who can be an opinion leader, even if he occasionally says the wrong thing. To become a leader one has to cross the desert in preparation. Our training is very intellectualized. That is, one understands that the reward system for party activists seeks out the brightest, those who can answer the toughest questions, for example, what Maritain said in one chapter or another, that kind of thing. But training also takes place in daily political activity, in your district or neighborhood. Those who have become leaders have done so because they have followed this road. To be a leader it is of key importance to be clear, to be at ease with oneself, to be sure of one's own identity."

As for the sector leaders, they are expected to struggle firmly for the demands and the rights of their sectors, but it can be said that, regardless of the respect aroused by leaders, they are all continually under observation and evaluation and activists on all levels are not shy when the time comes for criticism, although most of those interviewed did so in general terms, without mentioning names.

While it is obvious that leaders are "born," and then they develop and are "made" by practice, some of the more conspicuous and famous move up from their original groups and climb rapidly towards national leadership. One informant gives an example: "Ambrosio (Rodrigo) was a strong leader until 1972. He was an undisputed leader. He set up the network. He was a very charismatic leader—a man with a great deal of charisma. He brought lots of forward-looking people with him. Ambrosio is part of a set of people, at the University of Chile. He began to gather people around the Christian Democrat Youth to create a left wing revolutionary front."

Several informants indicated that the party also draws on those people who have certain qualities of a leader [*líder*], but are not full-fledged, and hence it calls them *dirigentes* [lower-level leaders]. An informant quoted earlier explains, "some are very good leaders [*dirigentes*] because they know how to express themselves well in public. They are also intelligent, but they are not of the same dimension. They are very good organizers, good students, good at proposing ideas within the party on anything in the technical field. There are very good leaders within the party. They are formed through training. Many have been union leaders, youth leaders at universities, in the university Federations, in unions, and so forth."

The emergence of leaders during the military dictatorship merits a section by itself. As one informant sees it: "In my day, in order to be a leader [*dirigente*] basically two things were required: we were in the midst of a dictatorship, and so audacity was required. A kid who could provide witness was an immediate leader [*lider*]; for example, he stood in the middle of the street and, suppressing his fear, made an accusation, and called for protest—that made him a leader. It didn't require a lot: audacity and the ability to string a few words together."

In this period peasant and labor leaders suffered many pressures and were harshly persecuted for their political ideas, for defending their sector interests, and their presumed participation in anti-dictatorship movements. Although organizations were broken and some fear was generated among the workers, new leaders emerged alongside those existing. "But the fear of repression meant that there was less of a pull to party activity, towards politics," said a rural leader. "I was put on trial by the dictatorship. I was found guilty by the dictatorship for being part of the aspirations of the people, of the peasants. The peasants told me that we had to ask for higher pay, more freedom to organize. I learned a lot from the young people, because they are very brave and very much want to change things. But I would tell them that more of them ought to join their organization. We have very good rural young people, but there aren't many."

A union leader also described the persecution: "I have been in prison several times since the beginning of the military dictatorship. I was arrested for being a leader of the United Workers Center. I belonged to the National Council and there was an order out to arrest all the leaders."

New social and economic developments have helped produce a new type of influential person within the party. They cannot be called leaders, at least not political leaders; they are technicians. Some informants even regard them as the opposite of the typical political leaders who run the party. A number of political analysts in Chile would like to see the development of what has been called a "transversal party," where activists would come from different parties and be united by their commitment to technical efficiency and a model of economic development that would pave the way toward a renewal-based "modernity." Some informants said that the Christian Democrat Party was losing its identity, and criticized it for maintaining continuity with the military regime in its economic orientation. At the same time, political formation has given rise to what some informants call a "political career," a notion associated with "clientelism," and the creation of machines within the party. Some informants called such leaders "operators." These developments have been very frustrating for activists. A younger generation informant who was an outstanding lower-level leader during the dictatorship states, "This is changing sharply with the coming of democracy. It has been very painful to young people who went into politics at this stage of the dictatorship, since personal example is no longer enough, much more political education is necessary. I believe that leaders are formed from the bottom. Young people, however brilliant, however wonderful their opinions are, are destined to failure, if they don't forge their career from below—e.g. from class leader and moving all the way up the line. The political career really does take place within the party. . . . What is typical of Christian Democrat leaders today is that they are great engineers in politics; they are extremely gifted at putting puzzles together. It's very hard to put together and get an agreement out of these guys; they have a hard time reaching agreement. It's a characteristic of theirs."

Thus, the leader-operators perform what this informant sees as an engineering job, as opposed to an old-style leader for whom charisma and the power to convince the masses were essential attributes. Today it is difficult to rally the masses, and rarely is a leader seen interacting with them, even with student masses. However, the role played by networks in the rise and continued support of leaders is still valid, perhaps more than ever. In this process some leaders rise above their primary network and enter higher ranks within the party itself, up to the top leadership.

For grassroots activists, leaders have to be constantly proving their leadership (as the notion of leader is commonly described). Thus, it can happen that they lose their power or ascendancy over the party masses. Some leaders who were doing well in their political careers suddenly vanished and were never heard from again; they left the party or they got stuck on the way. Other leaders who chose exile during the dictatorship have had to pay a heavy price for choosing to leave the country. "Some people have been left speechless. I have met really brilliant people within the party who suddenly disappear from the scene, perhaps for lack of political consciousness."

In any case, having followed a path within the party is apparently a necessary condition for those running for office in the name of the party.

Party Purity

Commenting on the concerns of Christian Democrat activists on present party identity, an informant, an outstanding second level leader, admits: "I feel that there is—rather than a fear of the Pact—a fear of our own loss of identity. People say: well, what is our identity? And this is the big question among Christian Democrats today. What are we going to do to distinguish us from the right and from the socialists? And continuing along these lines, she reflects: "I have the impression that this is reinforced by a certain long-standing culture in Chile, whereby it is difficult to relate to other parties, since each one tried to construct its own model and this model excluded the rest, because the point was to impose the model on the rest of society.

On the other hand, an old activist says, "People are very closed; they don't like more people joining. They are terrified that they will be invaded by people who may take advantage. There is always a difference between the old and the new. (. . .)

The party has had some recruitment campaigns; for example, when the legal parties became officially registered (when parties could become legal again during the military government) then they had an affiliation campaign. But the Christian Democrats didn't go out into the street to sign people up; we didn't put a sign-up table in the street. Rather people went to recruit among their friends, their relatives, acquaintances, neighbors who had inspired their confidence, perhaps coming out of church."

Stressing that there is a "difference between the old activists and the new," an informant exclaims, "It seems that people carry in their head not just a family genealogy but also a political one. The case of 'X' who, although he has been eighteen years in the party, is said not to be a Christian Democrat. What does that mean, that he doesn't come from a Christian Democrat family?"

To these references to the fear of "infiltration" into the party, or mistrust aroused by the entry of some new members, we can add this statement by one informant: "joining the party is something that you have to legitimize, step by step, a closed thing; one has to have been there from the beginning."

This suggests that the care for the purity of the party could be connected to a certain tendency to sectarianism on the part of the Christian Democrat Party, an impression frequently voiced by their adversaries and even by their political allies. Speaking of the election of Eduardo Frei Montalva (1964–1970) as the first president of the Christian Democrats, a party activist whose parents were then party activists, remembers the initial euphoria and then the subsequent disenchantment on realizing that in practice, the actions of many fellow party members were far from what ideological purity would imply: "There were attitudes of domination, struggles for positions; all the positions had to be for Christian Democrats." According to what they said, people of principle in the Christian Democrats left the party, like his parents. They continued to vote DC but they no longer participated in party life.

The Concept of Family in Christian Democracy

We begin a description of the characteristics of the Christian Democratic subculture with the concept of family. Among the DC, "the family is much more important than friendship," claims an interviewee.

Of the informants as a whole, one could say that most come from practicing Catholic families, or with a Catholic mother, whose influence contrasts with what we have seen in the Radicals, where the father appears to be the dominating figure. A well-known Christian Democrat, speaking of his approach to the ideas of Christian humanism, declares: "my mother had a profound effect on me; in those adolescent years, I didn't even know the Falange or the social-Christian movements existed. She was a very Catholic woman. . . . Besides, since she was a very intelligent woman, with a great capacity for argument and discussion, I ended up adopting her ideas and her example. That is the source of all my social-Christian tendency, even though during those years I never heard the term "Social-Christian." These were the seeds, to which I added my great concern for the government. This was what first affected me, and it was because of this that I joined the Catholic Youth and then went into politics."

A young mid-level leader remembers that his grandfather belonged to the Conservative Party, but that "my mother belonged to the new generation of socially-committed Catholics who decided to leave the Conservative Party and join the National Falange. She is an active Christian Democrat activist, and my father also."

The daughter of an eminent Christian Democrat leader states: "my father was the son of a Mason and a very Catholic mother." Another informant recalls that his maternal grandmother was "extraordinarily pious and generous." Both she and the grandfather "lived as very good Catholics," and his father was a soldier, non-active in (DC) politics until he retired from the army. But within the family, on the maternal side (uncles, mother) they were politically active. "All were voting Christian

Democrats." During the Popular Unity government, the Agrarian Reform provoked divisions in the family, among the Christian Democrats and with those on the right. His Christian Democrat grandfather lost some land. "It hurt him a lot, but not too much since that wasn't what he lived on." The grandfather's comment was "We lost our holiday home."

Another young woman declared that both her paternal and her maternal family were always connected with politics. "I am the daughter of a Christian Democrat. My father has always practiced politics from different points of view. Certainly at home I always heard that Maritain was important, that sharing was important, that solidarity was important . . . And we lived these values." The mother also shared these, although she was more to the right: "She has always been committed to public service." This informant is of the opinion that "in the Christian Democrat homes one feels 'guilt' more that in those to the left or the right. Actually, we are rather ashamed of owning material things. We are very austere."

To another, her maternal grandmother was a key person and she transmitted all the values of Catholicism to her family. Although she lived to see many of her grandchildren move to the left ("and she didn't like that") she was not upset enough to refuse to see them. "She was tolerant." In this informant's nuclear family she is the only Christian Democrat. "There is a bit of everything" in the sixty or so cousins of her generation. But during the Popular Unity many of those who were Christian Democrats went over to the right, for protection from the left. The paternal grandmother was very Catholic but her husband "had belonged to the Radical world." They only had boys and they were all very rich, and good-looking and had a "jet-set" style of life. The informant describes her mother's family as "typical Christian Democrat": Catholic with a "large social sense." She expresses the opinion that the cultural difference from the conservative sector that she came from began to become obvious in her own generation. "But they still sent their children to the same schools and they went to the same parties."

An informant who describes herself as middle class, tells how her parents became Christian Democrat activists when her father, an official in the civil police force, retired. She herself, a rank and file activist, put as a condition for her own marriage that she should be able to continue her involvement in politics (her husband is an independent leftist). In any case, the military coup considerably reduced her activity and her husband thought that she had become accustomed to the idea of living removed from politics. Nevertheless during the political activism of 1982 and 1983, there were conflicts. She worked in the protests (against the military regime), was president of a professional association in Region V. The risks worried her husband, who thought that she should be more committed to her children. But, to her, being involved with her children included working towards a better and more just world. Her children are still minors, the younger is "more Christian Democrat; the older one just observes." She thinks that they "will get there," in a natural way, through having lived certain principles. "They may not follow the Christian Democrat path, but they will have the same principles." Very much in contrast with the Christian Democrat families (and of Chilean family life in general), neither of her grandmothers played a central role in the family group. This tradition was revived by her mother and she continues it. She vigorously invokes the value of the family: "I believe that both in the highest and the lowest level, the concept of the family is the strongest thing there is."

Another informant who describes her family as very Catholic and very political declares that she, "feels like a sister to any Christian Democrat" even though they are not members of the party. Her father, a Conservative, became a Falangist, for which he "lost friends and suffered a lot." Her husband was totally Christian Democrat, "very committed internally." He worked in the campaigns but they had a hard time economically and they had to dedicate much of their energy to earning enough for their family of eight children. Two of their sons and three of their daughters are Christian Democrats. They have one son who is right wing and the rest are (not very committed) Christian Democrats. She says that her family is very united, but remembers painfully the discussions between her Christian Democrat children and her right-wing brother during the military government: "I stopped having Saturday lunches—we all got together on Saturdays—during the difficult times of the Pinochet government, which we were all against. I ended up crying sometimes because of the arguments. They argued, but they never fought. That is, they argued, but they went out together. They have always been very united. It's impressive."

Life-Style

Family once again plays the central part when we discuss the Christian Democrat life-style, since the Christian Democrat life-style is centered around family sociability, placing the accent on a sober, austere, simple life. Here again the social class of the informants, all Christian Democrats, has an impact. One of them, who is middle class, says that they got together on saints days, birthdays, and national holidays. As an example of the importance of these large family gatherings, another informant remembers that her mother invested all of her father's retirement money adding on to the house "with a large kitchen and a large dining room. She loved to see us all sitting around the table." When asked if her family had special culinary traditions she replied, "There were special customs, for example always on September 18th we ate *empanadas* (meat-filled pastry) and a chicken dish. My mother would have died if she hadn't done that." The other custom was to get together for saints days, "big parties."

By contrast, an upper class Christian Democrat remembers, "My grandmother thought it was bad taste to think too much about food. . . . We shouldn't talk too much about this. We didn't eat a lot, but it was very good food. The invited dinners were formal, nothing was improvised . . . we ate *centollas* (giant crabs), *guiso de panqueques,* beef, *corvina* (a fish), and desserts in fine dishes, those kind of things." This informant thinks that this world (hers) had more to do with class culture than with DC culture.

Another informant who is very committed to the idea of Christian humanism and is likewise of an upper-class background, invites all of the family on Saturdays. When asked if they ate a pre-set menu, she said: "No, I am only concerned that the food is good since my husband was quite a gourmet. . . . I inherited this from my mother, this idea of pleasing people through food. She used to prepare a lunch that was delicious, agreeable, with a pretty table, a pretty tablecloth." And what did they eat? "At home we ate very well, a *corvina* stuffed with shrimp and mushrooms, a fillet with good cream, eggs with sauce, lots of sauces, that kind of thing. But simple—how can I explain?—for example, in my mother's house we never had an aperitif." As far as inherited delicacies she says "I prepare a chicken mousse—my mother's recipe; my turkey recipe too; certain deserts that I have inherited (they came from an old family cook). My paternal grandmother's birthdays were always special celebrations, with lunch prepared by the cook, with turkey, three dishes, that kind of thing. We also spent Sundays at my grandmother's—on Sundays we had *empanadas* and pasta. There once again it was important to have a pleasurable meal, with a pleasant atmosphere . . . good wine, but all very sober. . . ." She insists on the importance of the aesthetic aspect. "The food was good, delicious, but it was very sedate."

Coming back to the middle class, an informant tells how the matriarch was her grandmother: "There were family festivals, very grand and happy, no politics. These were birthdays, saints' days. . . . The month of the saints was for dancing and eating." The grandmother preferred simple food, family food, very traditional, nothing extravagant. "But for her there could be no saint's day without turkey, without *empanadas*, these were made at any time of the year—enormous; wonderful dishes of turkey and chicken. Her grandfather (originally from Spain) loved meals "with lots of *chorizo* (Spanish sausage). "To make him happy grandmother learnt to make paella; she also knew southern cooking, *curanto* and *cocimientos*; she baked bread in her charcoal oven, every day; she made *pastel de choclo* (corn pie), *humitas* (corn pastries, like tamales), special creative salads; . . . an exquisite bread soup—cakes were not her strong point." Family life took place in the enormous kitchen of a large house in the country.

We have already mentioned an informant who believes that DC homes have strong guilt feelings about material things. She comments that in her home they were austere, but not tight-fisted. "That is," she says, "my mother said that two pairs of shoes was enough, three party dresses was enough." She herself feels strong twinges when she spends too much on clothes or in having a suit made. She observes that her right-wing friends can buy five pairs of shoes without batting an eye and walk out happily . . . "something which I, even although I have the money, I feel . . . I just can't."

Touching on another theme related to life-style a young female upper class Christian Democrat remembers that in her family they lived a regulated life: "what could be done, and what not; what could be said, and what not; it was all set down." Her father did not like them talking about politics or religion, preferring cultural topics. As far as the decoration of the house was concerned, her family avoided things that "were in bad taste" at all costs. Among these were decorations embroidered with crocheting. "Houses with these were the last thing one could tolerate in life." They also paid a lot of attention to table manners, and dressing properly. "I also insist on this," she adds.

In her well-off family it was the custom to send the children to Europe, or perhaps the United States, when they reached seventeen. Traveling was important. The interviewee remembers that her father would say "One has to get out of Curicó (a small provincial city). He considers that this is a life-style "almost identical to the conservative one." One difference is the areas where they choose to live; some live in Providencia or La Reina, the others (more to the right) live in La Dehesa (like many of their cousins). With her sisters she shares "the sense of dress, furnishings; furniture is the most important thing." Not only the furniture but also the pictures, fine china, crystal, cutlery. All this is valid even for their left-wing sisters. Changing this— "Oh no, that would be like changing one's soul." What does endure (in spite of political disagreements) "is the liking for certain good things." In her house, literature, cinema, and art were also important—music perhaps less so.

Repeating the emphasis on the family style of life, she recounts that every Friday she and her sisters and their respective children get together in their mother's house at 5 o'clock in the afternoon. Later the husbands arrive "and everyone talks."

More or less the same age (but middle class) is the informant who remembers her family gatherings. "They were very entertaining and we were very jolly." They got together with their cousins on their mother's side (who was the youngest of eight brothers and sisters). "My grandfather had land in the South; and when school ended all of us cousins went off there." In February the parents arrived, "We had a wonderful time," she recalls and adds, "I lived a country life with twin feelings, happiness for the experiences and pain for the hard work of the peasants. But grandfather and my uncle managed the land and were greatly loved by the workers. I realized that they did not have such an oppressed life as the left wing said."

The mother of this informant did not follow the tradition of these gatherings, as she did not have such a large house. "Besides" she suggests, "I think my mother resented not having gone to the university. She didn't work." According to her father "at this time it was not approved of (that the wife would work) it would be humiliating for him" and the interviewee comments, "male pride." The result is that the mother always said she envied her for being able to go to the university. Nevertheless she had a great family sense, "a bit like my grandmother" and organized gatherings for her parents' anniversaries, Christmas celebrations, lunches, (very austere, with 'a secret friend').[2] "I have a very matriarchal style," she says, "my

---

2. Game in which presents are exchanged.

brothers conduct their life around mine." According to her, politics destroyed their family life-style due to the conflicts between cousins (some were left-wing, some were DC, several went into exile). There were even some who withdrew from family gatherings because of the rule of not speaking about politics "at least not about current politics." She finishes by saying that the "coup ultimately split the family."

Reinforcing the idea of this family life-style is the testimony of one of the interviewees, the daughter and niece of members of congress: "It was a marvelous family life" (they spent every summer with the grandmother whom the grandchildren adored). The grandmother lived in the center of the city and every afternoon two of her sons, members of parliament, walked over from Congress. The adults sat on chairs, the children on the floor and they all listened to stories about parliament, about politics. "One drank in this ambience and politics as much as the older cousins."

At one time, "coming out" in society was the fashion for young females about seventeen or eighteen; never before. The life-style changed in the generation of their children, for example, the custom of going to parties accompanied by their father and mother. With the economic changes this informant was forced to give up her large house and ended up living in a very small apartment. But the inheritance of her husband was "marvelous: the generosity." Also in her family there was a lot of importance placed on furniture, paintings, and so forth, all of it bought "little by little." They also inherited things from their grandmother, from her parents, from the other grandmother. "It's very important to me that things are pretty, well presented," she says, "even though they are simple."

In contrast to the Radicals, we find in the Christian Democrat life-style not a common style due to a class (as among the Radicals and the middle class) but rather above all due to a shared Catholic social ideology which we mentioned at the beginning of this chapter. The upshot is that regardless of the informant's class, the accent is on austerity, sobriety, and simplicity.

Friendships

As already noted, the family is more important to Christian Democrats than friendship. Friendships normally occur from contacts made in school and the university and are connected to people with whom one has some political affinity. They are friendships that last and some participate in the DC social life. Nevertheless, some upper classes informants, who are likewise centered on a family-based social life, also have right-wing friends, "from before," "conservatives," with whom they continue to share a life-style.

"Our social life took place in the family," states an interviewee from this social stratum, and also in her husband's family which is right-wing, "very moderate, very generous, charitable, extraordinary in how they live to this day." However, she goes on to say that they also had DC friends "with whom we could agree more in our conversations," and people from the right as well, but "they were very sound people. The right-wing also has sound people, very serious, who also have wonderful customs. In other words, we didn't just socialize with DC people, not at all." Now widowed, she maintains her friendships with right-wing people—"different, but affectionate; they are old school friends, also wonderful people." She adds that when there is an election campaign she sees less of them. Since her husband was very generous, the house was always open and her children's friends were all welcome there. "My children's friends are from school and university." They also married within this environment. Not all of them are DC, and neither are the grandchildren.

A younger informant speaks of friends that "I stopped seeing during the dictatorship." She says that when she studied theater, she met many left-wing people but never established close friendships with them except for one, "a very good friend, a Communist." She adds: "I speak from my heart with left-wing people; with my friends from the theatre, I was more authentic. I felt perfectly understood, perfectly." Nevertheless, she has "right-wing friends" as well.

The friendships of another woman interviewed are "from the Catholic university world," very few from high school. The friendships from the Catholic University "are closely tied to the initial period of the opposition to Pinochet." According to a young informant, groups of friends of his generation meet "in different places, we get together in people's homes; we have had formal gatherings . . . to discuss matters; we have made agendas of issues to be discussed."

Recalling the period of military government, which she described as a "complicated period," another informant, not from the capital, says: "I was always interested in politics, and we began to form groups of friends and DC people and we began to share like a family. We went on outings to somehow keep analyzing the situation, which we couldn't do [publicly] at that time. So this was a procedure followed by many groups. Groups of friends, very close, but within the DC."

Here we can see that friendship among Christian Democrats is closely tied to political affinity, or directly to shared activism. There are some exceptions among upper-class informants who maintained their friendships with members of the same social sector, who were generally from the right.

Views of Others

Apparently due to the common denominator of Catholicism, the DC tends to compare itself more with the right, with conservatism, than with the left. "Look," says a district leader, "I don't have anything to do with someone from the right. I can tell you sincerely, beyond good friendly relations. . . . It's terrible because when you look at the right you can see that their only concern is to accumulate wealth and have a network of business-type organizations, with the bank, with transnational companies, and their world is all about money. All they defend is their personal interests. I find it a little cold towards society, since we Christian Democrats have always struggled for social equality." Another interviewee, very committed to DC ideology, declares: "The right was somewhat blind toward the dictatorship: they didn't want to see what was happening and defended their point of view as a defense against communism and naturally saw only the fear, seeing the terror, seeing the horror. That is, everything was justified for the sake of rescuing them in their situations. They are strong believers in "the faucet": to the extent that capital and capitalists are successful, it is going to trickle down to the people in need. I think that this is where the great difference lies. There is a difference of criteria in everything, living, thinking, and so forth."

Speaking of the ideals that unite all the DC, from whatever social stratum, she ends up accentuating "this opening up to love for humankind. That's how I feel," she says. "I feel it in the DC with people socially close to me, but I don't feel it deeply when I meet right-wing people; I tell you, someone could be a very good friend of mine from way back, who is right-wing, but when talking we avoid certain topics. Both of us do this, not just me. For example, I can't talk to her about the horror of Pinochet's government, which for me was the horror of horrors, while she thinks that it was stupendous since it saved us from communism. And they don't recognize all the positive things in communism, because, I swear, communism has given us positive things."

According to another interviewee, what separates the Christian Democrat from other groups with similar social ideas is the "Christian slant." She believes that the DC is "different from the conservatives, because ultimately Christian Democracy very clearly entails an option for the poor." For her, the Conservative Party has a paternalistic side. "For the DC, we are all equal," whereas the "others" have a "let's-give-this-poor-man-something" attitude. Nevertheless, she feels a great deal of respect for the Conservative Party, although it is a party that "offers top-down kind gestures, gestures that keep it from growing." This is the difference that she sees between the DC and the Conservative Party. "The agrarian reform made that quite clear," she maintains.

As for the Radicals, she views them as certain gentlemen who have gathered to eat at some club (the Radical Club). They meet there, they arrive at 3 o'clock in the afternoon and leave at midnight: "They eat a lot of meat, they drink a lot of wine." By contrast, what is important in the DC is "austerity, being measured." She sees the Radicals as "very fat" men. Nevertheless she thinks that the Radicals—"because they are centrists, may have been moving into the Christian Democratic Party."

Another difference with the Radicals is noted by an old activist who says "Of course we never use the word *correligionario* ["fellow believer"] which is a Radical term. We call one another "comrade" [*compañero*].

A provincial informant refers to the Radicals as "low class." She thinks that the Radical culture includes (Radical) clubs "but they are just bars, low class, disgusting." She says that in Region V the Radicals are "nowhere in sight." She considers them non-existent, "There's nothing serious holding them together." Except for one leader, she dismisses them as politicians to be taken seriously.

The last statement that we register presents a positive slant in the appreciation of the Radicals. A long time DC activist says, "We appreciate in the Radicals this pleasure that they take in life, very differently from the Christian Democrat leaders."

Concerns within the PDC

On the Chilean political scene today, the Christian Democrat Party is in a holding pattern. Since the return to democracy, it has won the presidency of the country twice, and it is far and away the majority political party. Nevertheless—or perhaps for that very reason—there is a great deal of introspection within the party and there are different tendencies or "sensitivities," some of them dating back quite some time, particularly grassroots concerns more about the ideological-cultural, than the merely ideological, characteristics of the party. These concerns reveal the contrast that activists perceive with their vision of themselves described above.

In the words of a PDC academic (verbal communication): "The interesting thing is to see this kind of 'cultural mass,' namely this party, which can lead to visualizing very conflictive internal relations. I think we could have very conflictive islands here. I think that putting this into words, giving it an empirical foundation, would enable us to find some policies for understanding. . . ." She sees a great risk in the Pact for Democracy: "I wonder if perhaps the modernizing elite aren't setting the pace, and whether there may not be a divorce between the top and the bottom, and that could be very disruptive."

A first complaint, one expressed publicly and that caused pain in the rank and file of the party, was that of former president Patricio Aylwin, who said he was afraid that the party "was becoming a springboard for getting jobs." The complaint may have been controversial but one informant provided support: "The party grassroots push, push, push. I think that it is how it was in the government of Frei (Montalva) [with pressures] in the party and in the government, to get jobs so . . . look . . . party culture. . . . you go to a party meeting and all you find is complaining." She is of the opinion that "there is a problem of internal communication; that is, nothing moves, there's no leadership, there's no information on the party, and that is one of the things that the party could do. There's no role for the party; there's no role for the parties in general. . . . Do you understand what I'm saying? People thought they were going to participate and they're not participating, because of the lack of leadership, because the parties are disoriented, because some went into the government, and some went into parliament, but the parties have been left without many internal functions."

Jaime Castillo, the well known proponent of Christian Democrat ideology, states in a press interview: "the president (Aylwin) and many others are giving warnings about the same things. How can this be resolved? In my opinion, there should be a radical change of procedure within the DC, so that a political leader can provide a different kind of example. That's why I think that we must talk about these things now, not hide them, because to hide them would entail falling into the same mistakes."

Replying to the question as to whether "this personalistic shoving" existed at the beginning of the PDC, Castillo answers:

"No, it used to be a lot less; in fact people had to be pushed to take jobs, as opposed to this expectation of people for jobs. . . . For example, the discussion of the candidature of Cruz-Coke or Gonzalez Videla was marvelous because of the underlying issue and because of the way the leaders treated one another, with a close friendship, although their positions were in opposition. All these things constituted a school, namely the Falange, and I think that we should return to that, that we should always try to reproduce it as much as possible."

Sharing this nostalgia is a former district leader who says. "We were more disciplined at the beginning . . . and there were fewer of us. The tasks assigned were in fact orders; there were fewer distractions; with the party and the church you had plenty." A young man comments: "at the ideological congress it seemed like something new that we [the young people] were all in favor of the human being . . . and it seemed revolutionary, something new. The older folks said 'How wonderful this congress of young people is, what nice things they said.' But we're not saying anything new, we're just recalling what we seem to have been forgetting." Another young man says in confirmation, "We have to get back to a utopia, we can't remain pragmatic; a young party is one that has utopias."

Another activist claims that there are internal fights, that there is "little solidarity within the party in Santiago." There are arguments, and above all, the leaders "impose the authority consistent with their political position." Moderating his complaint, he says that he thinks it is connected with "the evils of a large city," and that "it is the behavior of a population rather than of a party." Nevertheless, he insists that at election time people offer their votes in exchange for other things (for the community, of course). "That is, there is a relation between you wanting to be a parliamentary member, and you wanting me to help you, we make a deal for the vote, independently of the interest of the community, the interest of my country, above the concern for having members of parliament who can legislate well, with laws that are just and fair and promote equality and solidarity." At election time, he says, the people become active but "they ask for things as if there were a bottomless barrel," he concludes.

To another informant, a regional director, the worrisome thing is the discrepancy between principles and the life-style of some Christian Democrats. "Nowadays, there are a number of Christian Democrats that it's painful for me to say that they are DCs, because of the way they are and the way they act. . . . They don't fit," he says. Illustrating this discrepancy, he states that there are those who say they are for human beings, but they use their authority very harshly. They are concerned about productivity, they fire people, they don't even know what is happening with their families, and so forth. "It's either useful to them or not." He adds that there are others who are consistent with their principles. Hence, the fact that some are "rotten" does not invalidate everything.

With respect to comparisons with the way things used to be, he believes that there used to be figures who were weighty, who led upright lives, who were consistent and had principles, values, capabilities, and that that was why they emerged as leaders due to their very solidity, and "the kinds of things that happen now didn't happen then." Today there is a shortage of leaders, leaders like that who were above reproach. "Now politics seems to be more about groups than personalities." She misses leaders of a more solid type who could offer a living model of their doctrine. There is a need for someone imposing, against whom nobody can compete, who brings about agreement above everything else and "who is capable of more enthusiasm." She gives as an example of this lack of enthusiasm the fact that in the last election for the party president, when Foxley won, "nobody got worked up." In her opinion "the pragmatic approach doesn't produce excitement, nor an enthusiasm leading to sacrifice." She believes that this is not happening in the church either, where there is also a lack of leadership, adding that the church's attitude "drives young people away."

This informant does not believe in factions. She thinks that they arose out of the different positions taken to confront the dictatorship (some in favor of civil protest and others who thought the solution lay within the established institutions) and time showed who was right. She thinks that the factions respond to personality cults rather than underlying issues, although she recognizes that there were real issues between the *chascones* (long-hairs, intellectuals) and the *guatones* (fat cats, who enjoy a comfortable life-style). "Nowadays," she says, "different groups are kept going not by ideological or strategic differences but out of friendship, teams. . . ." She does not want to be classified. "Nowadays the differences are not legitimate ones; now they are for reasons of power, but not underlying issues." With regard to the "Frei-ist" and "Aylwin-ist" tendencies, she believes that they result from the tendency "not to take our legacy and go on from there, but rather to destroy and start from zero, in order to appear important." In her opinion, this practice has broken up teams and has been disastrous. She speaks of a *chascon* leader whom she regards as inconsistent in his attitude and not very conciliatory: "I think that one can change things without having to get into fights with everyone . . . because you can change things by convincing others rather than through confrontation . . . A politician should fight over content, not form."

Certainly, one of the most painful aspects in the PDC now is the problem of internal elections, designating candidates, and assigning positions (for candidates of the various elections) within the Pact for Democracy. In one informant's opinion, the party bleeds in internal elections: "A lot of us are wounded on the battlefield." She says she feels afraid because the fights are "squabbles" over tiny pieces of power. She feels this wears the group down instead of building it up. Nevertheless, she states that in the face of any situation (of crisis or danger) the party would "unite fiercely." The PDC spirit continues and it is "as in family clans." She is also worried about the lack of new leaders. The existing ones are traditionalists and "set, we could say, in families." As far as she has been able to see, "there are people who maintain—I don't dare to do this, since I actually don't believe it's true—but there are comrades who maintain that unless your name is Aylwin, or Frei, or Saldivar, or Valdes, you're no one in the party. So a Perez, a Muñoz, a Gonzalez is lost. I feel this is not so true." In any case it is her perception that the people of her generation, who are middle aged, "aren't anywhere." She believes that the campaign slogan for Frei (Eduardo Frei Ruiz-Tagle, the current president) is particularly telling: "new times." She says: "I don't know what they had in mind with the slogan but for me the new times have signified a rather destructive style of politics." She points to a degree of authoritarianism, citing cases of a change of minister or of the director of Television Nacional. She considers that at her level this new style is very unacceptable. Her generation, people of forty to forty-five years of age, were accustomed to debate. That is why people "are into something that has much more to do with ego," and that has undermined the party at the grassroots.

Without referring expressly to currents or sensibilities, this informant speaks of "machines," and believes that they still exist. "There are people committed to people in the party; people who get jobs by being friends of a governor, or a mayor, and so forth. . . . The delegates arrive at a meeting already "sewed up" and "don't want to hear, or read, or debate anything." Their commitment is not one of friendship but is job-related, economic, and has to do with clientelism "This was not done in the party until 1970." She thinks that this grew during the dictatorship because of the difficulty in getting together and holding elections. "Those who could organize things became established. They were not all deserving, but 'tricks were played.'"

(The lament of a young leader fits in well at this point, to be followed by the opinions of the same interviewee. The young man said: "You realize that you end up sacrificing your life and you begin to question it. In other words, is it worthwhile getting rid of the dirt in order to end up depending on the machinery that will expel you?")

Referring once again to the "fight" for positions (on the ballot) the interviewee says "it is ferocious." She says she is herself a *chascona* (intellectual), but believes that the Aylwin government was excellent. She accepted it because she was used to debating. "Today divisions are sharper. There is no longer any deep conversation; in internal elections people get stuck in one tendency or another." She adds that there are many people like her, who have sat down to think and who conclude that open, not closed, leadership is necessary. She accepts the market economy "but with a social balance." She cries out that poverty is a world disgrace, and says that Chile "is not even on the way to development." To her the important thing now is that the Pact not be broken. "We have to create a new kind of mystique, grounded in our earlier mystique."

An interviewee, a district leader, believes that "those down below stay below," and that even though they prove themselves capable as grassroots leaders "they are not appointed. . . . That is what is going on now." There is a gap between the top leadership and grassroots leaders. "Because if you ask me why . . . how come you never find a grassroots woman occupying any ministry? [The comrades] feel hurt."

A statement by another leader at a similar level reinforces this idea: "My female comrades have told me that in this regard they feel put down and frustrated. This is really a pity." She adds: "There's one thing I don't agree about. Do you know what? I think that the comrades who are given important jobs should be closer to the grassroots. Look, what are people complaining about? That they see very little of their top leaders and they would like to be closer to them, have a closer dialogue with them, see more of them. This is not because they want to get things out of them, but they want to listen to the words of guidance, wisdom, knowledge, that we all really need at some time or another."

In conclusion, we can appreciate certain characteristics in the ideology and behavior of the DC that shape its subculture. The most important features, and those that set them apart from Radicals are their desire to maintain the purity of the PDC ideology and the selectivity of the group, the importance that they attribute to their leaders and their level of morality, the importance of family above friendship, the role of the Christian mother, and the precedence of personal moral values over the role of the party in social matters.

5

Conclusions

The aim of this study has been to test a theoretical model proposed by the authors for analyzing and understanding Chilean political culture by means of an examination of history complemented by research based on open-ended interviews, participant observation, and work in newspaper archives. This model combines a structural analysis based on social networks (horizontal and vertical) with the description of the symbol system that provides them with feedback. In this sense, political culture is the grammar of the relations of domination, subordination, and cooperation; in other words, the grammar of power and how it is expressed.

We find that Chilean society is horizontally structured in social classes, within which are found informal social networks that may for ideological reasons become formalized in political parties, composed in turn of different networks arising out of friendship, within generational cohorts, and groups based on regional origin, family, neighborhood, school, parish, association, or shared interests. The informal groups exercise a certain control over their members. Although these networks are horizontal in nature (with the characteristic element of trust) they identify their own leaders, but such leadership is conditional. In other words, a leader who attempts to act beyond the group's wishes, or who arrogantly tries to impose a style of vertical leadership without consulting them immediately causes rejection on the part of network members and they withdraw their trust in him as leader. On the other hand, there are leaders who cross network boundaries to reach higher levels of leadership within the party. There are others, who precisely for not having managed to reach these higher levels while having managed to maintain the trust of their group, create tendencies first and then factions within the party, thereby ultimately leading to the creation of a new political group.

By briefly reviewing Chilean history, one can see that political groupings represent different social classes, but just as significantly they manifest ideological differences over the religious question and its relation to the state. That is why we chose to study two parties that are essentially middle class, but that differ in that one has a militantly secular character, greatly influenced by Masonic principles in its development (the Radical Party) and the other is very closely linked in its growth and political action to the Catholic Church (the Christian Democrat Party).

Thus, within the structure of horizontal networks belonging to the same social class, one can distinguish ideologically differentiated networks, which form parties, which in turn develop processes of cultural identification, and that exhibit their own life-style. This is what we have called the party subcultures. It is interesting to note that these groups maintain certain cultural boundaries that separate them from other groups but nevertheless continue to sustain their Chilean character. It is worth mentioning that both parties share the characteristics of Chilean political culture with reference to the structures of the social networks, horizontality and verticality, conditioned leaderships, family life, and so forth, while displaying clear differences in their symbol systems (values, discourses, ideology, life-styles, and so forth).

It may be noted that the Christian Democrat Party (PDC), which was conceived as a middle-class party, has maintained its cultural connections with the upper class (because it emerged from the Conservative Party) and in the 1960s it succeeded in becoming a multi-class party by drawing in many agricultural workers and poor city dwellers. This presented a problem for analyzing the data obtained in fieldwork, because the life-styles of the DC activists interviewed varied according to their social class. (The problem did not arise in the case of the Radicals.) They are alike, however, in the type of Catholicism that they practice, their (Christian humanist) values, their discourse, and how they see themselves.

The study began with an overview of the nineteenth and twentieth centuries which provided the basis for the theoretical model of the characteristics of Chilean political culture. In it we can see that the Conservative Party, the first party to emerge after Independence, was the product of a dissatisfaction of the "aristocratic fronde" with the president's authoritarian behavior. Later, and with the rise of another network of the same aristocracy—the Liberal network—ideological differences about involvement of the church in state affairs began to appear. The upshot was the emergence of the Liberal Party, from which the Radical Party split because of disagreements over the issue of religion. The Radicals were emphatically secular, anticlerical, promoters of secular education, and advocates of the free thought, positivism, and humanism of their French counterparts, and were supported by Freemasonry. All these principles, plus the socioeconomic changes in the country during the last third of the nineteenth century, made the Radical party the champion of the incipient Chilean middle class. In this historical example one sees how new horizontal networks break off from older ones and become distinct from them and go on to embrace a different ideology, largely because of changes in economic development of the country and the role which the new network goes on to play in that development.

In the twentieth century the middle class expanded enormously because of the need for mid-level people to serve in the army, develop nitrates, serve in government and the educational system, and so forth. The liberal professionals needed for such development were a product of state-run education and that was the foundation for the power of the Radical Party. The popular urban sector, which had already taken root in the twentieth century because of the country's economic development, was also a basis of support for the emerging Radical Party, which served as an intermediary between the dispossessed classes and the national oligarchy. In the first half of the twentieth century, with three Radical presidents in a row, the Radical Party laid the foundations for the country's industrialization, sponsored the expansion of the public education system, and became involved with health care, all of which caused the state apparatus, and with it the Radical Party, to grow.

Meanwhile, Marxist parties appeared on the left and began to represent the urban proletariat. These parties were rooted in ideology as well as class. As the influence of Marxism rose in Chile and in the world, the Catholic church put more emphasis on offering an ideological alternative in defense of the poor, with the Church's social doctrine as expressed in the papal encyclicals. This doctrine was adopted in Chile as the basis for the social thinking of Catholic student networks, which were eventually absorbed (as ANEC) by the Conservative Party and continued to develop there until they become the Falange. They later left the Falange over ideological differences that led to a definitive split (conservative church vs. social church). When this network finally formed the PDC, once again a portion of the Conservative Party (the Social-Christian network operating there) split from the main body and joined the new Christian Democrat Party. This new party therefore had within it two networks with different social origins. Nevertheless, the ideologically dominant group was the Falange, which offered the Catholic middle class an opportunity to be politically active in accordance with their religious principles. Furthermore, with its ideology of social justice, it sought to attract not only the middle class but also the peasantry and the urban proletariat. It had become a multi-class party, but was united by a strong political and religious ideology which would be the basis for the development of its subculture.

THE SUBCULTURES

The study of the subcultures of the two political parties involved in this work clearly confirmed the original hypothesis of differentiated party subcultures. Although both parties generally represent the middle class, and have held similar positions on the role of the state in society, their basic ideological differences (secularism vs. Christian humanism) have attracted different social groups from the beginning. For example, the PR originally developed in provincial groups, and its customs, life-styles, and sociability reflects a certain kind of provincial life. By contrast the Falange, which gave rise to the PDC, began with Catholic intellectual university groups in Santiago, whose less gregarious and more austere and moralistic life-style imprinted a character on the group. Hence, we see that the provincial-style sociability of the Radicals and their egalitarian and non-sectarian ideology, with a heavy emphasis on friendship, is also reflected in their formal and informal organizations: the open assembly as its basic organ of political sociability, with the Radical Club as the main place for coming together. By contrast, the main realm of DC sociability is the family, and in terms of formal party organization they have their district-level grassroots organizations which are closed to all but party activists.

Whereas from the beginning Radicalism emphasized tolerance, conciliation, its "Chilean identity," the ability to negotiate and its broadmindedness, the Christian Democrat Party, in its formative period, proposed as a doctrine that it had a way of its own, thereby basically implying a corresponding tendency to exclude others. So they are even reluctant to admit new activists, especially at the grassroots. In their discourse, the interviewees expressed this in terms such as "fear of the new members," "fear of infiltration," "need for legitimacy within the party," mistrust of what are called "interlopers," and so forth.

On analyzing the discourse of each party, one can see a different accent, a specific way of talking, and a vocabulary that expresses the values that each regards as important.

Radical discourse places the accent on the party's great achievements in Chilean history: the secularization of some public institutions (Civil Registry, cemeteries); the implementation of the idea of the "Teaching State," and the establishment by the state of an infrastructure to modernize the country (for example, the creation of CORFO (Corporation to Aid Production). In addition, a central part of the Radical discourse is the theme of friendship: helping one's friends "of all colors," the conviction that Radicals are good friends, and even putting friendship above political questions. In their discourse, as it appears in the interviews, Christian Democrats do not refer to party achievements on behalf of the country (although they exist), but by contrast, their discourse is essentially axiological, based on an "ought-to-be" that is shared by grassroots activists, mid-level leaders, and national leaders. It is an imperative to be generous, supportive, a good father, good mother, one who struggles for social justice, and austere in one's life-style (in food and clothes). The criticisms Radicals level at their party have to do with the political actions of their leaders, such as having made an alliance with the right, or having supported the Law for the Defense of Democracy, or any other political mistake they may have made. However, they have no critical attitude towards *amiguismo* (friendship) or *compadrazgo* (cogodparenthood), which most of them accept, dismissing the suggestion that this practice might be blameworthy. Indeed, they justify it on the grounds that friends should help one another, and friends do not exclude friends of another political inclination. The critical discourse of Christian Democrats toward their party is closely linked to the imperative of the PDC "ought-to-be" described earlier, and is directed at both the grassroots and the upper levels of the party. Political mistakes by PDC leaders were rarely mentioned in our interviews.

One last noteworthy difference that we will point out between the two subcultures refers to the effect of the mother or the father on their children in their adoption of the corresponding political culture. In the case of the Radicals, it was the father, without exception, who was the central figure and the most influential in the choice of political path adopted by the children, even though many had mothers who were practicing Catholics. By contrast, among the Christian Democrats we interviewed, it was a socially concerned Catholic mother who was the bearer of a doctrine aimed at carrying out such principles. It should be emphasized that the sociability of the Radicals occurs most often outside the home, in male groups, whereas Christian Democratic sociability is centered more at home, in the family where the mother can exercise a greater formative and centralizing influence, and it is she who takes her children to mass.

In summary, through our fieldwork we could clearly distinguish a "Radical" culture and a "Christian Democrat" culture. We think that these cultures or subcultures have more weight in the development and the permanence of each party and endure longer in time than the principles of political ideology. Even though the different parties that make up the Pact for Democracy (governing coalition) have accepted the currently prevailing model for running the country, with its ingredients of globalization and neo-liberalism, and de-emphasis on class struggle, there nonetheless persists a collective conscience with its symbolic boundaries. What now distinguishes each from its coalition partners is its subculture and the fact that they recognize themselves as different and see others as different.

Bibliography

Almond, Gabriel (1990). "The Study of Political Culture." In G. Almond, ed., *A Discipline Divided*. Newbury Park: Sage Publications.

Almond, Gabriel, and Sidney Verba (1963). *The Civic Culture*. Princeton, N.J.: Princeton University Press.

Alonso, Jorge (1996). "Cultura Política y Partidos en México." In Esteban Krotz, ed., *El Estudio de la Cultura Política en México (perspectivas disciplinarias y actores políticos)*, pp. 187–214. Mexico: CNCA/CIESAS.

Barth, Frederick (1969). *Ethnic Groups and Boundaries*. London: Allen & Unwin.

Blau, Peter (1964). *Exchange and Social Power in Social Life*. New York: John Wiley and Sons.

Boizard, Ricardo (1965). *La Democracia Cristiana en Chile*. 2d edition. Santiago de Chile: Editorial Orbe.

Castillo, Jaime (1973). *Teoría y Práctica de la Democracia Cristiana Chilena*. Santiago: Editorial Del Pacifico.

Coppedge, Michael (1997). "A Classification of Latin American Political Parties." Kellogg Institute Working Paper.

———. (1997). *The Evolution of Latin American Party Systems: Democracy, Politics and Society in Latin America. Essays in Honor of Juan Linz*. Boulder, Colo.: Westview Press.

Dittmer, Lowell (1977). "Political Culture and Political Symbolism." *World Politics* 29: 552–83.

Drake, Paul (1978). *Socialism and Populism in Chile*. Urbana: University of Illinois Press.

Donoso, Ricardo (1952). *Alesandri, agitador y demoledor.* Mexico: Fondo de Culture Economica.

Edwards, Alberto (1982). *La Fronda Aristocrática.* 8th edition. Santiago: Editorial Del Pacifico.

Edwards, Alberto, and Eduardo Frei (1949). *Historia de Los Partidos Políticos Chilenos.* Santiago: Editorial Del Pacifico.

Enriques Frodden, Edgardo (1994). *En el Nombre de una Vida.* Mexico: Universidad Autónoma de Xochimilco.

Fleet, Michael (1985). *The Rise and Fall of Chilean Christian Democracy.* Princeton, N.J.: Princeton University Press.

Garretón, Manuel A. (1987). *Reconstruir la Política,* chaps. 4 and 5. Santiago: Editorial Andante.

———. (1993). "Cultura Política y Política Cultural." In Manuel Antonio Garretón, Saúl Sosnowski, and Bernardo Subercaseaux, *Cultura, Autoritarismo y Redemocratización en Chile,* pp. 223–34. Santiago: Fondo de Culture Economics.

Gazmuri, Cristián (1991). *El "'48" Chileno. Igualitarios, reformistas, radicales, masones y bomberos.* Santiago: Editorial Universitaria.

Gomez Oyarzún, Galo (1989). *Origen y Desarrollo de la Universidad en Chile.* Mexico: Ediciones Casa de Chile en Mexico.

Góngora, Mario (1981). *Ensayo Historico sobre la Noción de Estado en Chile en los Siglos XIX y XX.* Santiago: Editorial La Ciudad.

Lomnitz, Larissa (1971). "Reciprocity of Favors in the Chilean Middle Class." In *Studies in Economic Anthropology,* complied by George Dalton. Washington, D.C.: American Anthropological Association.

Lomnitz Adler, Larissa (1975). *Cómo Sobreviven los Marginados.* Mexico: Siglo XXI.

Lomnitz Adler, Larissa, and Marisol Perez-Lizaur (1987). *A Mexican Elite Family.* Princeton: Princeton University Press.

Lomnitz Adler, Larissa, and Leticia Meyer (1988). *La Nueva Clase.* Mexico: UNAM.

Lomnitz Adler, Larissa, and Ana Melnick (1991). *Chile's Middle Class.* Boulder: Lynne Rienner Pub.

Loveman, Brian (1988). *Chile: The Legacy of Hispanic Capitalism.* 2d ed. New York: Oxford University Press.

Mainwaring, Scott, and Timothy R. Scully (1995). "Introduction. Party Systems in Latin America." In Scott Mainwaring and Timothy R. Scully, eds., *Building Democratic Institutions: Party Systems in Latin America,* pp. 1–34. Stanford: Stanford University Press.

Martínez Javier, and Eugenio Tironi (1985). *Las Clases Sociales en Chile.* Santiago: Ediciones Sur.

Michels, Robert (1969). "Los Partidos Políticos." In *Estudio Sociológico de las Tendencias Oligárquicas de la Democracia Moderna.* 2 vols. Buenos Aires: Amorrortu.

Moulian, Tomas, and Torres Dujicin, Isabel (1990). *Discusión entre Honorables.* Santiago: Flacso.

Nuñez de Pineda and Francisco Bascuñán (1973). *Cautiverio Feliz.* Santiago: Editorial Universitaria.

Panebianco, Angelo (1990). *Modelos de Partido.* Mexico: Alianza Editorial.

Polanyi, Karl (1957). *Trade, Market, and Early Empires.* New York: Free Press.

Pye, Lucien (1972). "Culture in Political Science: Problems in the Evaluation Concept of Political Culture," *Social Science Quarterly* 53: 285–96.

Radcliffe-Brown, A. R. (1952). *Structure and Function in Primitive Society.* London: Cohen and West.

Remmer, Karen (1984). *Party Competition in Argentina and Chile: Political Recruitment and Public Policy, 1890–1930.* Lincoln: University of Nebraska Press.

Sartori, Giovanni (1980). *Partidos y Sistemas de Partidos, Marco para un Análisis.* Madrid: Alianza Editorial.

Scully, Timothy, (1992). *Los Partidos de Centro y la Evolución Política Chilena.* Santiago: CIEPLAN-Notre Dame.

———. (1995). "Reconstituting Party Politics in Chile." In Scott Mainwaring and Timothy R. Scully, eds., *Building Democratic Institutions: Party Systems in Latin America*, pp. 100–37. Stanford: Stanford University Press.

Sepulveda Chavarria, Manuel (1994). *Crónicas de la Masonería Chilena.* Vol. 1. Santiago: Ediciones de la Gran Logia de Chile.

Serrano, Sol (1994). *Universidad y Nación: Chile en el Siglo XIX.* Santiago: Editorial Universitaria.

Stallings, B. (1978). *Class Conflict and Development in Chile, 1958–1973.* Stanford: Stanford University Press.

Tironi, Eugenio (1985). *La Clase construida I: Apuntes acerca de la producción simbólica de la clase media.* Working Paper No. 53: SUR.

Urzúa, G. (1986). *Historia política electoral de Chile, 1931–1973.* Santiago: Tomarcoa-Van.

Valenzuela, Arturo (1977). *Political Brokers in Chile: Local Government in a Centralized Polity.* Durham, N.C.: Duke University Press.

———. (1989). *El Quiebre de la Democracia en Chile.* Santiago: Flacso.

Valenzuela, J. Samuel (1985). "Democratización vía Reforma: la expansion del Sufragio en Chile." Buenos Aires: IDES.

———. (1995). "The Origins and Transformations of the Chilean Party System." Kellogg Institute for International Studies Working Paper #215. December 1995.

Vial Correa, Gonzalo (1981). *Historia de Chile (1891–1973).* Vols 1–3. Santiago: Editorial Santillano.

Yocelevzky, Ricardo (1984). "La Democracia Cristiana Chilena: Trayectoria de un proyecto." Typescript.

———. (1987). *La Democracia Cristiana Chilena y el Gobierno de Eduardo Frei.* Mexico: UAM Xochimilco.

Index

Agrarian Labor Party, 57
agrarian reforms, 59, 107–8
Aguirre Cerda, Pedro, 39–40, 54, 86
Alessandri, Arturo, 38, 42, 45
Alessandri Rodriguez, Jorge, 43, 61, 111
Alfonso, Enrique, 56–57
Allende, Salvador, 43–44, 63–66
Almond, Gabriel, 3
Alonso, Jorge, 15
Ambrosio, Rodrigo, 117
amiguismo, 101–3, 146. *See also* patronage
ANEC (National Association of Catholic Students), 47–53, 144
ANOC (National Association of Peasant Organizations), 61
anti-clericalism, 22, 28–30
anti-communist organizations, 61
Aranda, Fidel, 49
Araucanian Indians, 23
aristocracy: and the Catholic Church, 24, 38; expansion of, 22; and Liberals/Liberalism, 25, 28; political influence of, 17–21, 143

Arteaga, Justo, 30
ASICH (Chilean Union Action), 60, 61
assemblies, electoral, 31, 33, 40–41
Assembly for Conservative Propaganda, 50
Atacama Fraternity, 31
Atacama Liberal Party, 31
authoritarianism, 6, 7, 9
authority, principle of, 19
Aylwin, Patricio, 70; administration of, 72–73, 106; austerity of, 114; and PDC, 59, 134

"Barber's Congress," 55
Barth, Fredrick, 10
births, registration of, 22
Bolivia, 23
Borgono, Barros, 37
Bossay, Luis, 43, 85
bourgeoisie, 29, 32, 33–34, 37. *See also* middle classes
broadmindedness, 94, 100
brotherhood, 35, 41, 94
Bustos, Manuel, 70

"cabinet of social sensitivity," 56

Caesarism, 18, 20–21

Campos, Jaime, 86–87

Castillo Velasco, Jaime, 58–59,
 134–35

Catholic Action, 47, 49

Catholic Church: and ANEC,
 47–51; and the aristocracy, 24,
 38; and emergence of political
 parties, 22; and human rights
 under military dictatorship,
 70; Jesuit political influences,
 47–49, 59, 60–61; and
 Marxism, 60, 144; and PDC,
 60, 112–13, 129

Catholic University, 39, 49n1

cemeteries, secularization of, 22, 92

Center for Conservative Students,
 51–52

Center of Social Development for
 Latin America (DESAL), 61,
 110

Centro Bellarmino, 61

Chilean '48, 24–25, 48

Chilean Union Action (ASICH),
 60, 61

Christian Democratic Council, 56

Christian Democrat Party (PDC),
 11, 43, 47–79; and Allende
 administration, 63–66; and
 ANEC, 47–53; and the Catholic
 Church, 60, 112–13, 129; and
 Christian democracy, 57–60;
 concerns within, 133–39;
 dissolution of, 70; and education, 39, 110; electoral reforms
 of, 56; factionalism in, 61–62,
 64–65, 78, 136–37; and the
 FN, 47, 53–57, 58; formation
 of, 9, 24, 47, 57, 144; and Frei

administration, 60–63; ideology
 of, 113–15; leadership in,
 74–79, 116–20, 137–38; and
 Liberals/Liberalism, 113; and
 Marxists/Marxism, 113; and
 the middle classes, 58, 109,
 111; and military dictatorship,
 67–74, 118; networks in, 39,
 76–79; and peasants, 59–60,
 111; purity of identity in,
 120–21; Radicals' views on,
 107–13; social classes in, 58–60,
 65–66, 77, 82, 109, 111, 125–29,
 142–43; structure of, 74–79,
 137–39; subcultures in, 113–39,
 145–47; U.S. impact on, 62

Christian Democrats: austerity of,
 114; and enjoyment of food,
 125–27; and families, 122–29;
 and friends, 109, 130–31;
 life-style characteristics of,
 113–15, 125–29, 136; mothers'
 ideological influence on, 122,
 147; and "ought-to-be," 114,
 146; views on other groups,
 131–33; views on Radicals,
 132–33

Christian Democrat Youth, 117

Christian Land Federation, 60

Christian Left Party, 65, 73

church-state relations, 22, 28–29,
 46, 92, 142

clientelism, 138

Cobo Alemparte, Santiago, 30

Communist Party, 40; electoral
 force of, 45, 72; expelled from
 government, 43, 56; Radicals'
 views on, 110, 112

Communists/Communism, 61, 63,
 70, 109

compadrazgo, 102, 146

Concepción (city), 18, 35

Conservative Party, 143; and ANEC, 50–52, 144; and the FN, 53–55, 144; ideology of, 22; sectarianism of, 24

Conservatives/Conservatism, 23, 32; factionalism of, 21; landowners' alliance with, 62; Liberal Party, alliance with, 28–29; PR's alliance with, 43

Constitution of 1833, 20

Constitution of 1980, 67, 71

Copiapó (city), 31, 35

corruption, political, 56, 102–3

Creoles, 17

Cruz-Coke, Eduardo, 55, 57–58

deaths, registration of, 22

Delpiano, Victor, 49

democracy, compromise-based, 107

Democratic Party, 42, 43

DESAL (Center of Social Development for Latin America), 61, 110

development, 58–59

discourse, 146

Dittmer, Lowell, 4

Doctrinaire Radical Party, 43

Duhalde, Alfredo, 43

Duran, Julio, 43–44

Economic Commission for Latin America (ECLA), 59

education, 24; foreign influences in, 39, 84; Montt's reforms of, 22–23; and PDC, 39, 110; and PR, 37–40, 83–84, 88; and Radicals' work-study relationship, 99, 108. *See also* schools

Edwards, Alberto: on the aristocracy, 17, 18, 21–22; on the liberal fronde, 22; on "liberal religion," 25; on O'Higgins, 18, 20; on Portales, 19; on power structures, 19–20; on the Radicals, 27

egalitarian networks, 7, 77

electoral assemblies, 31, 33, 40–41

electoral reforms, 56

encyclicals, social, 47–49, 60

English influences, 23

Enlightenment, 19, 28

entertainments, 96–97

Errazuriz Zañartu, Federico, 29, 42

exchanges, 5–11

Eyzaguirre, Jaime, 49

factionalism, 7–9, 24, 78–79; of Conservatives/Conservatism, 21; in FN, 55; and friends, 79; of Liberals/Liberalism, 21; in PDC, 61–62, 64–65, 78, 136–37; in PR, 41–45

families: and Christian Democrats, 122–29; as horizontal networks, 17; Masonic lodges as, 36, 105; in Mexican social structures, 6–7; as proto-parties, 21; in provincial life, 96; and Radicals/Radicalism, 95, 99–100

fathers, ideological influence of, 100, 105, 122, 146

Ferrando, Ricardo, 55

fire fighters, 25, 32, 36–40

Fleet, Michael, 63–66, 69, 71

FN. *See* National Falange

foreign influences, 23, 28–29; in education, 39, 84; and fire

foreign influences (*cont.*)
  fighters, 36; and Freemasonry,
    34
FRAP (Popular Action Front), 61
FRAS (Radical Agrarian Socialist
    Falange), 56
Freemasonry, 25; and PR, 34–36,
    38; and Radicals/Radicalism,
    32, 41, 83, 88–89, 91, 102, 105
Frei Montalva, Eduardo: agrarian
    reforms of, 59; and ANEC,
    49, 51; and Assembly for
    Conservative Propaganda,
    50; austerity of, 114; and
    Conservative Party, 52; and
    the FN, 55; growing influence
    of, 57; and Marxists/Marxism,
    63, 65; "No" campaign in 1980
    plebiscite, 67, 71; opposition
    leadership of, 65, 69; and PDC,
    58, 59, 60–63; PDC views on,
    121, 134; on political parties,
    45–46; on PR, 38; presidential
    election of, 44; Radicals' view
    of, 108, 110–12; reforms of, 59,
    62; senatorial election of, 56
Frei Ruiz-Tagle, Eduardo, 70, 73, 138
French influences, 23, 28–29, 34
friends, groups of: and *amiguismo*,
    101–3, 146; in Chilean social
    structures, 6–7; and Christian
    Democrats, 109, 130–31; and
    factionalism, 79; as horizontal
    networks, 17, 77; as proto-
    parties, 21; and Radicals,
    96–97, 100–103
Fuentealba, Renan, 65, 68

Gallo, Angel Custodio, 29, 30
Gallo, Pedro Leon, 29

Garretón, Manuel Antonio, 16, 64,
    65
Garretón Walker, Manuel, 50–51,
    53–54
Gazmuri, Cristián, 32n1; on fire
    fighters, 37; on Freemasonry,
    35–36; on Liberals/Liberalism,
    30; on political sociability,
    24–26, 48; on PR, 29, 31
generation-linked networks, 77–78
"generation of 1825," 24, 28
German influences, 23, 28, 84
Góngora, Mario, 19, 20, 22
Gonzalez Videla, Gabriel, 40, 43,
    55–56, 86
grammar, cultural, 1–2, 10–11, 141
Group of Ten, 69–70
Gumucio, Rafael, 55
Gumucio, Rafael Agustín, 50, 57, 59
Gumucio, Rafael Luis, 50, 52

Hales, Alejandro, 58
Hamilton, Eduardo, 49
Hamuy, Mario, 58
hierarchy. *See* leaders/leadership
historical background, 17–26
horizontal networks, 2, 5–11,
    141–42; aristocratic fronde
    as, 19; and families, 17; forma-
    tion of, 143; and friends, 17,
    77; and leadership, 24, 78–79,
    119–20; and political parties,
    22, 45, 77
Humanist Party, 73
human rights, 70

Ibañez, Carlos, 42, 43, 111; authori-
    tarianism of, 9; dictatorship of,
    50, 58; presidential election of,
    57; strikes against, 49

identity: group, 81–82; national, 19,
24; party, 120–21
individualism, 48
informal networks, 24–26, 76–77,
81, 141. *See also* Radical Clubs
Institute of Christian Humanism,
113
Institute of Rural Education (IER),
61
institutionalization of political
parties, 13–15
International Congress for Catholic
University Students, 51
Irureta, Narciso, 59, 65

Jerez, Alberto, 59
Jesuit influences, 47–49, 59,
60–61

Lagarrigue, Javier, 49
Lagos, Ricardo, 73
laicism, 37–39, 89, 92
landowners, 59, 62
Larson, Oscar, 47–49
Latin America, political parties in,
14–15
Lavanderos, Jorge, 58
law, respect for the, 11, 92
Law for the Defense of Democracy,
43, 56
leaders/leadership, 6, 7–9, 141–42;
and horizontal networks, 24,
78–79, 119–20; in PDC, 74–79,
116–20, 137–38; in PR, 85–87
leftists, 64–65, 106
legitimacy, principle of, 11, 17–18,
20, 24, 75
Leighton, Bernardo, 55; and
ANEC, 49; and Assembly for
Conservative Propaganda, 50;

government posts held by, 52,
54, 56; opposition leadership
of, 65, 68
Leo XIII (pope), 47
Letelier, Valentin, 37, 42
Liberal Party, 143; alliance with
Conservatives, 28–29; ideology
of, 22; *pipiolos* in, 18; sectarianism of, 24
Liberals/Liberalism, 27–30, 32;
factionalism of, 21; as parliamentary fronde, 22; PDC as
alternative to, 113; PR's
alliance with, 43; and
social/economic changes, 23;
and the younger aristocracy,
25, 28
life-styles: of Christian Democrats,
113–15, 125–29, 136; of
Radicals, 82–87, 96–105
Lomnitz, Larissa Adler, 6, 7
Lorenzini, Emilio, 60
Loveman, Brian, 60

machines, political, 78, 138
MacIver, Enrique, 42
Mainwaring, Scott, 14–15
Mardones, Jorge, 57
Marin, Francisco, 30
market exchanges, 5
marriages, 22, 92, 93
Marxists/Marxism, 60, 63, 65, 113,
144
Masonic lodges. *See* Freemasonry
Matta, Guillermo, 30
Matta, Manuel Antonio, 30–32
Maza, Lorenzo de la, 49
men: and sociability, 35, 37, 147;
suffrage for, 22, 29
Mexico, 6–11, 15, 19

middle classes: expansion of,
143–44; and FN, 54, 55; and
PDC, 58, 109, 111; and PR, 38,
42, 113; and provincial life,
96–97; rise in, 23, 38, 83–84.
See also bourgeoisie
military dictatorship period, 67–74,
118. *See also* Pinochet,
Augusto
model for study of political culture,
1–2, 10–11, 46, 141
modernization, 48, 51, 58–59, 134
Montt, Manuel, 22–23, 28–29, 37
mothers, ideological influence of,
122, 147
Moulian, Tomas, 64, 65
Movement for Peasant Liberation,
60
Movement of Popular and
Unitarian Action Party
(MAPU), 62, 64, 78
Musalem, Jose, 58
mutual aid, 103, 105

National Association of Catholic
Students (ANEC), 47–53, 144
National Association of Peasant
Organizations (ANOC), 61
national character, 82–84
National Conservative Youth
Movement, 52
National Coordination of Unions,
70
National Falange (FN), 53–57, 60,
144; factionalism in, 55; and
middle classes, 54, 55; and
PDC, 47, 58; in Santiago, 145
National Institute, 37
National Internado, 37
nationalism, 19, 24

negotiation, 12–13, 41–45, 75–76,
105
neighborhoods, 98
networks: egalitarian, 7, 77; exchange, 5–11; horizontal, 2,
5–11, 17, 19, 22, 24, 45, 77–79,
119–20, 141–43; opposing
Allende government, 64–65;
social, 2, 5–11, 46; vertical, 2,
5–11, 78
non-governmental organizations,
61

O'Higgins, Bernardo, 18, 20
"operators," 76, 78, 119

Palacios, Nicolas, 37
Palma, Ignacio, 56
Panebianco, Angelo, 12–14
parliamentary systems, 7, 21–22
Parties for Democracy Pact, 72–74,
87, 105, 134
Party for Democracy (PPD), 44,
72–73, 92
patronage, 62–63. *See also*
amiguismo
patron/client exchanges, 5, 11
PDC. *See* Christian Democrat Party
peasants, 56, 59–61, 111, 118
pelucones, 30
People's Democracy, 43
Perez, Clemente, 49
Perez, Jose Joaquin, 27, 32
Peru, 23
Philippi, Julio, 49
Pinochet, Augusto, 9, 44, 72. *See also*
military dictatorship period
pipiolos, 18
Pius XI (pope), 47–48
Pius XII (pope), 47, 60

Poblete, Renato, 61
Polanyi, Karl, 5
political culture, 2–4; model for
    study of, 1–2, 10–11, 46, 141
political parties: and continuity
    given by subcultures, 10; group
    identity in, 81–82; historical
    background of, 17–26; and
    horizontal networks, 22, 45,
    77; institutionalization of,
    13–15; multiplicity of, 45; and
    social networks, 46; studies
    of, 12–16. *See also names of*
    parties
political styles, 105–7
Popular Action Front (FRAP), 61
Popular Front, 39
Popular National Party, 57
Popular Socialists, 43
Popular Unity, 63–66, 105–6
Portales, Diego, 19–21
positivism, 22–23, 28
power structures, 12–13, 19–20
PR. *See* Radical Party
Pradel, Fernandez, 47
Prado, Benjamin, 65
presidential systems, 6, 20
proletariat, 38, 45
Pro-Peace Committee, 70
proto-parties, 21
provincial life, 96–98
PRSD (Radical Social-Democrat
    Party), 44, 74
Pye, Lucien, 4

Radcliffe-Brown, A. R., 6
Radical Agrarian Socialist Falange
    (FRAS), 56
Radical Clubs, 33–40, 89–95, 96,
    97–98

Radical Party (PR), 11, 27–46;
    alliance with Liberals and
    Conservatives, 43; and *amigu-*
    ismo, 101–3, 146; as arbitrator
    of Chilean democracy, 106–7;
    and corruption, 102–3; and
    education, 37–40, 83–84, 88;
    factionalism in, 41–45; and
    the FN, 60; formation of, 9,
    24, 30–31, 143–44; and
    Freemasonry, 34–36, 38; fu-
    ture of, 44–45; and laicism,
    38; leadership in, 85–87; mem-
    bership of, 33, 38; and the mid-
    dle class, 38, 42; negotiation
    in, 41–45, 105; networks in,
    88, 100–101, 103–5; and
    Parties for Democracy Pact,
    72; and Popular Unity, 106; and
    Radical Clubs, 33–40, 89–95,
    96, 97–98; and the Society of
    Equality, 25, 32–33; structure
    of, 25, 40–41; subcultures in,
    82–113, 145–47; and the work-
    ing class, 42
Radical Social-Democrat Party
    (PRSD), 44, 74
Radicals/Radicalism, 27–33;
    Christian Democrat views
    of, 132–33; dress styles of,
    98–99; and enjoyment of food,
    97–98; and families, 95, 99–100;
    fathers' ideological influence
    on, 100, 105, 122, 146; and
    Freemasonry, 32, 41, 83, 88–89,
    91, 102, 105; and friends, 96–97,
    100–103; landowners' alliance
    with, 62; life-style characteris-
    tics of, 82–87, 96–105; Matta's
    principles of, 30; as middle

Radicals/Radicalism (*cont.*)
    class culture, 113; neighbor-
    hoods for, 98; political style of,
    105–7; views on PDC, 107–13;
    work-study relationship of,
    99, 108
reciprocal exchanges, 5–7
re-distributive exchanges, 5
reductionism, psychological, 4
Reform Club, 25, 32, 34
reforms, 22–23, 56, 59, 62
religion. *See* Catholic Church;
    church-state relations
Remmer, Karen, 21, 31
respect for ideas, 95, 100
Rettig, Raul, 43, 106
Reyes, Tomas, 49
Rios, Juan Antonio, 40, 55, 86
Rios Valdivia, Alejandro, 88, 104
Rodriguez, Pedro J., 55
Rodriguez Velasco, Luis, 30
Rogers, Jorge, 55
Roman, Pastor, 49
Ross, Gustavo, 54
Ruiz Tagle, Alfredo, 49
Rural Catholic Action, 61

Sanchez, Manuel Francisco, 49,
    50, 55
Santa Maria, Domingo, 49
Santa Maria, Jaime, 49
Santiago (city): aristocracy con-
    centrated in, 17; and FN, 145;
    and Freemasonry, 35; and PR,
    31, 98; as social center, 18–19
Sartori, Giovanni, 12
schools: as PDC social networks,
    39; as PR social networks, 88,
    100–101, 103–5. *See also*
    education

scientism, 28
Scully, Timothy R., 14–15, 28,
    30, 74
sectarianism, 24, 93, 111, 121
secularism, 24, 28, 30, 37–38,
    91–93
Silva Bascunan, Alejandro, 49
Silva Cimma, Enrique, 44, 85
Silva Solar, Julio, 59
sinecures, 62–63
sociability, 32, 33–40, 48, 77; po-
    litical, 24–25, 29, 31. *See also*
    social networks
Social-Christian Conservative
    Party, 57
Social-Christians, 47–51, 53, 58, 122
social classes, 6, 11, 46, 81–82,
    141–42; aristocracy, 17–22,
    24–25, 28, 38, 143; bourgeoisie,
    29, 32, 33–34, 37; middle, 23,
    38, 42, 54, 55, 58, 83–84, 96–97,
    109, 111, 143–44; and PDC,
    58–60, 65–66, 77, 82, 109, 111,
    125–29, 142–43; peasants, 56,
    59–61, 118; and PR, 38, 42, 82;
    proletariat, 38; workers, 42, 48
Social Democrat Party, 40, 44, 85
social encyclicals, 47–49, 60
social inequalities, 60
Socialist Party, 45, 63, 70, 72–73, 92
social networks, 2, 5–11, 25, 141;
    and political parties, 46; and
    proletarian subculture, 45; and
    radicalism, 33–40, 88–113.
    See also sociability
Society of Equality, 25, 32–33
Sole Worker Federation, 70
Spain, 17–18
speech, cultural, 1, 11, 146
strikes, 49, 69

structures, social. *See* social
    networks
student movements, 47–54, 55–56,
    144
subcultures, political, 81–139,
    142, 145–47; and Christian
    Democrats, 113–39, 145–47;
    and continuity, 10; and
    Radicals, 82–113, 145–47
suffrage, 22, 29, 56
Sule, Anselmo, 44, 85, 86–87
symbol systems, 2, 5, 82, 142

"teaching state," 24, 39–40, 84, 146
technicians, 118–19
tolerance, 44, 93–94, 100
Tomic, Radomiro, 49, 50, 55, 65,
    111
trust, 6, 8, 66, 78, 141–42

uncertainty, zones of, 13
Union of Christian Peasants, 61
unions, labor, 69–70, 104, 118
United States, 62
University of Chile, 36, 39, 84

Valenzuela, Arturo, 7
Valparaiso (city), 34–35, 36
Vekemans, Roger, 59–61, 113
Verba, Sidney, 3
vertical networks, 2, 5–11, 78
Vial, Camilo, 21, 30
Vial Correa, Gonzalo: on entertain-
    ment in the middle classes,
    96; on Freemasonry, 36, 103,
    105; on national unity, 24; on
    PR, 31; on public education, 38
Vicariate of Solidarity, 70
Vives, Fernando, 47
vote buying, 56

Walker, Horacio, 57
War of the Pacific, 23
Wartemberg, Sergio, 87
"we-ness," 10, 14, 64, 115
woman suffrage, 56
workers, 42, 48, 69

youth movements, 52, 62, 117

zones of uncertainty, 13